Father and Mother and boys with
The Brethren, 1934

Tony in Home Guard
uniform,
aged seventeen

DARE TO BE A DANIEL

Tony Benn was first elected to the House of Commons in 1950 and retired in 2001 'to devote more time to politics'. He is the longest serving Labour MP of all time and has held senior Cabinet and party posts. In 2002, the year after his retirement, he was voted Politician of the Year by Channel 4 viewers.

He is the author of many books, including his powerful case for constitutional change, *Common Sense* (with Andrew Hood), *Arguments for Socialism*, *Arguments for Democracy* and eight volumes of diaries.

Tony Benn has four children and ten grandchildren. He was married for 51 years to Caroline, socialist, teacher and author, who died in 2000.

Praise for the Benn Diaries:

'An astonishingly moving and human document' – Anthony Howard, *Sunday Times*

'A powerful record of the times' – Simon Heffer

'The best political diarist of our time' – Malcolm Rutherford, *Financial Times*

'The Benn Diaries, intensely personal, candid and engaging as they are, rank as an important work of historiography' – Alan Clark, *Daily Telegraph*

'Immensely readable and revealing' – Ben Pimlott, *Sunday Times*

'The finest reporter of political events in recent memory' – *Sunday Express*

DARE TO BE
A DANIEL

THEN AND NOW

TONY BENN

Edited by Ruth Winstone

arrow books

First published by Arrow Books in 2005

1 3 5 7 9 10 8 6 4 2

First published by Hutchinson in 2004

Arrow Books
The Random House Group Limited
20 Vauxhall Bridge Road, London SW1V 2SA

Random House Australia (Pty) Limited
20 Alfred Street, Milsons Point, Sydney
New South Wales 2061, Australia

Random House New Zealand Limited
18 Poland Road, Glenfield
Auckland 10, New Zealand

Random House (Pty) Limited
Isle of Houghton, Corner Boundary Road & Carse O'Gowrie
Houghton 2198, South Africa

The Random House Group Limited Reg. No. 954009

www.randomhouse.co.uk

A CIP catalogue record for this book is available
from the British Library

Papers used by Random House are natural, recyclable products made from
wood grown in sustainable forests. The manufacturing processes conform to
the environmental regulations of the country of origin

Typeset by Palimpsest Book Production Limited,
Polmont, Stirlingshire
Printed and bound in Great Britain by
Bookmarque Ltd, Croydon, Surrey

ISBN 0 09 947153 1

Contents

Illustrations

Family sailing
Mother and Father at Stansgate
Boys with Olive Winch
Benns on active service 1940
Westminster School bombed 1941
Family photo 1943

Second Section

TB as Private, Pilot Officer and Sub-Lieutenant 1942–45
Fairchild Cornell and Airspeed Oxford planes
'Wings' parade
TB meets Caroline 1948
Caroline and Tony Crosland
TB and Caroline at Stansgate
Caroline on car
Caroline on day of wedding 1949
Beautiful bride
Nurse Olive with Stephen
The family in Cincinnati 1959
The special bench 1979
Caroline's gravestone at Stansgate
TB and Speaker Martin 2001
Family photo 2003

*Unless otherwise attributed, all the photographs are from the
author's collection*

Acknowledgements

Writing this account of the influences, incidents and events which shaped my early childhood and growing up has been a challenging experience. It has allowed me to recall a comfortable but austere world in which my family was rooted in dissenting non-conformity, radicalism and commercially successful Victorian enterprise. But in the background was an awareness, while I was still a small child, of international danger looming.

The book serves as a prelude to the eight volumes of published diaries which together cover my life as I approach eighty. It was my son Joshua who first suggested that it should be written, proposing *The Weetabix Years* as a title because it conveyed the idea of a happy family at breakfast.

This became the working title and I wrote to the Chairman of Weetabix for his agreement; Sir Richard George replied to re-assure me on that point but felt he ought to tell me that Weetabix was not available when I was born.

'Dare to be a Daniel, Dare to stand alone' was the advice my dad gave me and was a phrase that greatly influenced my life, and it became the title.

The book owes much to Ruth Winstone, the editor of all the volumes of my diaries. I merely provided the raw material. She cross-examined me on it, clarified the ideas, and tried to unravel family anecdotes, myths and relationships. Working with her has been a real pleasure over the course of nearly twenty years. Jessie Fenn worked on the first draft with good humour, and Mandy Greenfield and Mary Chamberlain helped greatly on the manuscript, copy-editing and proof-reading with care and attention to detail.

I must also thank my brother David and his wife June. David's phenomenal memory has provided missing dates and incidents, and June, as a writer, provided valuable guidance on structure and content. To my own family I owe a great debt for their unending love, support and advice, the more so since my wife, Caroline, died in 2000.

Tony Whittome of Hutchinson has devoted much of his own time to this book and indeed my publishers have become good friends, in particular Emma Mitchell, my publicity 'minder' who has guided me through the mysteries of the literary world.

Tony Benn
June 2004

Part One

My Faith

Honest Doubt

I was born in 1925 into an Edwardian household influenced by Victorian values. Although I enjoyed a degree of security and privilege denied to most people, I was also the child of radical, nonconformist parents, and life at home was shaped by a tradition of austerity lightened by my father's sense of fun. Writing this book about my childhood, and its domestic, family and political events and experiences, has led me to examine how these elements combined during my growing up in the inter-war years to determine my character and beliefs.

The discipline of recalling childhood events and memories, and the origins and development of my own faith, has also helped me to analyse more specifically than ever before the nature of my belief, and why and how my views have developed over the years.

One of the most significant aspects of my childhood was my mother's deep Christian convictions, which she hoped her children would share, and I often forget that few people now have a biblical background or knowledge of the different Christian traditions. Biblical and religious references that slip into my speeches and articles are not necessarily always understood.

Leaving the moral teaching and theology aside, the one characteristic of most religions when they become established – and certainly of Christianity – is the entrenchment of authority at their heart, with the Pope at the centre of the Roman Catholic Church and the Archbishop of Canterbury at the heart of the Anglican community, each in their time having great power over their respective churches and enforcing the Christian doctrine, sometimes ruthlessly, as at the time of the Inquisition and on other occasions when heretics were burned at the stake.

This authoritarianism, and the hierarchy that supports it, seems to be inherent in any faith when it develops in an organised form. The Stalinist dictatorship in Russia showed that this characteristic is not confined to religion, but can apply to other belief systems as well – in the case of the Soviet Union, supposedly the teachings of Marx.

The Labour Party itself, which was inspired by men and women of principle, became corrupted by the same power structures, leading to the expulsion of difficult people on the grounds that they were not prepared to accept orders from the Party hierarchy; sectarian socialists can also develop in a way that discourages and represses dissent, just like religious sects forever fighting each other.

This attempt to control what people think and say has been – and still may be – so oppressive and brutal that inevitably there have always been individuals who rebelled against it and argued that they had the right to think for themselves. Such people were generally excommunicated, expelled or even hanged, and therefore few of them ever had any political power; but they had huge influence. The teachers who explained the world without wanting to control it themselves have always played an important part in the development of ideas.

Indeed, my mother, when she read me Bible stories, always distinguished between the kings of Israel who exercised power and the prophets of Israel who preached righteousness, and I was brought up to believe in the prophets rather than the kings.

This dissenting tradition lies at the root of Congregationalism, in which my father had been brought up as a child and which my mother adopted after rejecting the Church of England, with its discrimination against women.

Dissenters think for themselves and claim the right to do so, even in matters of faith. The 'priesthood of all believers' is based on the belief that every person has a direct line to the Almighty and does not require a bishop to mediate concerning what to believe and what to do.

This of course was, and remains, a completely revolutionary doctrine because it undermined authority, disturbed the hierarchy and was seen as intolerable by the powers that be, in exactly the same way that, today, political dissenters are projected as trouble-makers and members of the 'awkward squad', whose advice would lead to chaos. The fact that dissenters may be right is ignored, although history often shows that their views may turn out to be the conventional wisdom of the generation that follows them.

Since the control of people's minds is even more important than the physical control of society by the use of police and military repression, those who challenge the ideas that are being imposed are seen as a threat in political as in religious matters. During the Stalinist period, Soviet dissidents were treated very harshly by the Kremlin, but were of course welcomed by the anti-communist world, which hailed them – not necessarily because of agreement with what they said, but because their ideas were seen to be destabilising the enemy during the Cold War.

As I get older, I realise that the right to think for yourself and say what you think is an integral part of the renewal of all systems. It gives those who are victims of those systems some hope that there is a better way of running the world.

Though my father was in no sense a 'pious' man, he was a dissenter and the one characteristic that illuminated his life was his support for the underdog and a passionate commitment to freedom, justice, independence and democracy, a commitment that he must have inherited from his family, notably his grandfather Julius Benn, who was a Congregationalist minister.

Julius set up a refuge for destitute boys, in a disused rope factory in the East End of London, in the course of trying to reflect that passion for justice in a practical way. When Charles Dickens visited the hostel, he said of Julius, 'One could see by the expression of this man's eye and by his kindly face that Love ruled rather than Fear, and that Love was triumphant.'

Julius's son John (my grandfather) interpreted that commitment by political work and, as a founder member of the London County Council, contributed towards the development of municipal socialism, which enormously improved the prospects of people in London at a time when education and health were run by a series of unaccountable, corrupt boards.

As a Member of Parliament representing an East End constituency, my own father, William, was deeply involved with the Trades Council in its struggles for justice, and he always saw his role there as being pastoral in character.

My mother, Margaret, joined the Labour Party at the same time as my father, but confined her work to the elimination of injustice within the Church, especially in arguing for the rights of women, in seeking to eliminate anti-Semitism and in maintaining the principle that chapels should elect their own ministers and not have them imposed from above. But she was not so directly concerned with other forms of social injustice.

Indeed, there are two ways of looking at the moral responsibility that the dissenting tradition imposes. One is the charitable approach, whereby those who are better off assist the poor and devote themselves to that work wholeheartedly and sincerely. The other is one that attempts to tackle these same problems politically, by identifying the causes of poverty and trying to correct them through institutional and political changes that bring about a better state of affairs.

Historically those who complained of the injustice of the world would be assured by their Church that they would get their reward 'in heaven'. This, though very welcome, led some people to respond by asking why they could not have their reward while they were still alive!

The idea of Heaven on Earth – or justice in practice – was an integral part of the dissenting tradition and of the trade-union movement, which recognised that you could only improve conditions by your own collective efforts; and the Christian tradition in socialist thinking was combined with the strength of the trade unions.

Having been protected throughout my life from any direct experience of poverty, and having been to schools where this did not touch on any of the families, I came to understand trade unionism and socialism by experience during the war and, afterwards, as an active constituency Member of Parliament. It was only through those experiences that I came to see the importance of what I had been taught as a child in a rather theoretical way – independence of mind.

The first example in my own life of swimming against the political current of the time occurred in respect to appeasement. The boys at school, with one or two exceptions, supported Neville Chamberlain, and earlier were very sympathetic to Franco during the Spanish Civil War. Because of what I had heard at home, I was resolutely opposed to appeasement and argued the evils of fascism, of which I had very little knowledge although, as a boy of ten, I did see Oswald Mosley, a one-time colleague of my father in the Parliamentary Labour Party, marching through Parliament Square with his men in black shirts. And I was with my dad, in my early teens, when he addressed a meeting in the East End that was attacked by the Blackshirts and we had to leave the stage in a hurry.

The second example of conventional wisdom that I came to question was during the war itself, when it was quite obvious that there were two wars going on at the same time, which – although they coalesced in the desire for victory – were differently motivated.

The motivation of the British establishment in the 1930s was to thwart the spectre of communism in Britain and Europe. However, during the war, the Left thought it was fighting fascism and did not see the conflict in national terms; after all, there were many Germans fighting fascism in their own country who were our natural allies.

We now know that there was a debate going on in the government right up until the spring of 1940, considering the possibility of a deal with Hitler. The arrival of Rudolf Hess in May 1941 was obviously a last-minute attempt by Hitler to win over British support for his attack on the Soviet Union. At that time Senator Harry Truman (later President) made a statement that if the Russians seemed to be winning, we should support the Germans; and if the Germans seemed to be winning, we should support the Russians – in the hope that as many as possible would kill each other.

Right up to the end of the war Hitler was telling his own people that the Nazis were fighting communism.

After the war the conventional wisdom that dominated the Cold War period was that communism was a *military* threat, which was thought more likely to influence the public mind than an ideological threat to capitalism, which was what governments really feared. I came to realise that the USSR never planned to overrun Western Europe.

In retrospect, I see the Cold War hysteria as resembling the relentless pursuit of an enemy in earlier years, when those who challenged the conventional wisdom of the Church were seen as enemies of society and were regularly persecuted.

The liberation movements in the colonies were also presented as posing a threat to civilised society, and those who led them were vilified, arrested and imprisoned. They included some of the most distinguished world statesmen, such as Nehru, Gandhi, Nkrumah, Jagan, and of course Nelson Mandela.

Yet young men who went into the colonial service to become adminstrators (some of whom I knew) did approach their task with a sense of duty inspired by a moral responsibility that God had imposed upon them – such was the belief in imperialism as a force for good.

Today we are being asked to accept a new conventional wisdom, which is that America has assumed the same imperial role that Britain once exercised, in a crusade against a new threat of terror closely associated with the Muslim world. The use of the word 'crusade' by President Bush gave this battle the same sort of religious authority that persisted in religious wars in the past.

In parallel with this we have had the counter-revolution against the welfare state, trade unionism and democracy. This was launched during the Reagan-Thatcher period and was motivated by the realisation that politically-conscious trade unionism operating within a party with socialist roots was capable in a democracy of changing the balance of power permanently and peacefully, and that too was completely unacceptable.

Margaret Thatcher could herself claim non-conformist roots, and in some ways traced her ideology to the Manchester School of Liberalism associated with Mr Gladstone; but her interpretation of rugged individualism was that the enemy was the state, from which individuals had to free themselves.

My mother's dissenting Congregationalism was interpreted quite differently. She was a very devoted and serious Christian and gave me a grounding in both the Old and New Testaments of the Bible; we prayed together at night, and I went to St John's Church in Smith Square, where Canon Woodward (later Bishop of Bristol) conducted children's services. I was as devout as could be and took very seriously the obligations of Holy Communion after I was confirmed.

On the wall of my bedroom I had a painting of one of King Arthur's knights praying at an altar on the evening before he was admitted to the Round Table. That image influenced me subliminally as I grew up, in feeling that my boyhood should be used to prepare me for my work in life, which I was vaguely aware would be 'in the public service'. My mother once gave me a tiny Crusader cross, which I wore round my neck with my RAF identity discs throughout the war, and still have at home. It was not until much later that I realised how brutal the Crusaders were in their determination to seize the Holy Land from the heathen, murdering and maiming the people who lived there.

Another picture, 'The Boyhood of Raleigh', showed a young man with an old sailor pointing over the distant horizon, helping him to form in his mind the idea that there was a world to be explored. Both pictures made a great impression on me.

One of the stories my parents were fond of was that of Daniel who, having refused to give up his faith when tested by Darius, the King of Persia, was placed all night in a lions' den and was found the next morning unharmed.

Father used to recite a Salvation Army hymn, 'Dare to be a Daniel, Dare to stand alone, Dare to have a purpose firm, Dare to make it known'; those lines lodged in my mind so that, whenever the going has been rough, I have fallen back on it. It has taught me the importance of consistency and courage in the face of adversity – essential for anyone who is criticised for his convictions. In 1983 I saw in the YMCA in Nagasaki, of all places, a picture of Daniel standing with his hands behind his back and his head bowed, surrounded by the lions. I photographed it and it hangs in my office to remind me of those qualities that are the most important in public life:

Standing by a purpose true,
Heeding God's command,
Honour them, the faithful few!
All hail to Daniel's band!

Dare to be a Daniel,
Dare to stand alone!
Dare to have a purpose firm!
Dare to make it known.

Many mighty men are lost
Daring not to stand,
Who for God had been a host
By joining Daniel's band.

Refrain

Many giants, great and tall,
Stalking through the land,
Headlong to the earth would fall,
If met by Daniel's band.

Refrain

Hold the Gospel banner high!
On to vict'ry grand!
Satan and his hosts defy,
And shout for Daniel's band.

Refrain

Mother was scholarly, but she did not take a fundamentalist view of the Christian message or ever say or do anything that encouraged me to rebel. My brother Michael, who wanted to be a Christian minister after the war, set up his own prayer circle at school, and I drew great comfort from the knowledge of God watching over us. When I learned to fly, my mother told me that 'underneath were the everlasting arms', implying that even if I crashed, I was in the hands of the Almighty.

When my brother died in his plane, I found great comfort from praying for him and went to see the chaplain at the base in Africa where I was stationed to talk about it.

But, over the years, imperceptibly my faith has changed. I certainly was not influenced by atheistic arguments, which were extreme and threw doubt on the value of the Bible and the historical truth of Jesus's life, and which mocked religious leaders, whose life of service entitled them to respect.

Inevitably a greater understanding of science, not least Darwin's *On the Origin of Species*, played some part in undermining the idea that a kindly God and his Son could possibly have founded the universe, with billions of stars in our galaxy and billions of galaxies beyond us, whose origins could hardly have been explicable in that way.

But the real reason why my faith changed was the nature of the Church and the way in which it sought to use the teachings of the Bible to justify its power structures in order to build up its own authority.

For example, the idea of original sin is deeply offensive to me, in that I cannot imagine that any God could possibly have created the human race and marked it at birth with evil that could only be expiated by confession, devotion and obedience. This use of Christianity to keep people down was, I became convinced, destructive of any hope that we might succeed together in building a better world.

Of course what it did do was give the priests power over us, by hinting darkly that if we did not do what they told us to – and give money to the Church – we would rot in hell. Many of the hymns and prayers that I know and love contain ideas which have the same effect, and I came to repudiate them completely.

This did not in any sense involve accepting the implicit atheism of Marx, but when he spoke of religion being 'the opium of the people', it seemed to be a statement of my belief, without in any way demeaning the importance of the teachings of Jesus.

Indeed, I came to believe that Marx was the last of the Old Testament prophets, a wise old Jew sitting in the British Museum describing capitalism with clinical skill, but adding a moral dimension. *Das Kapital* could easily have been written in a completely factual way, describing exploitation as a part of the normal pattern of capitalism, without expressing any moral judgement on the matter. But Marx added a passion for justice that gave his work such unique political and moral power.

Also, the older I become, the more persuaded I am that organised religion can be a threat to the survival of the human race, and is fundamentally undemocratic in its structure and basically intolerant of those from other faiths, whom it sees as threatening its claim to contain the truth.

Political leaders can harness religious prejudice to justify their own policies and help sustain them in power, by claiming to speak with authority on behalf of those simple teachers who founded the religions which they purport to espouse. This is as true of President Bush and the Christian fundamentalists as it is of Osama bin Laden.

The 'opium of the people' exactly describes fundamentalist Muslims, evangelical American Christians who claim that God is on their side in a new crusade, and those Jews who believe that the Almighty granted them the right to own Palestine, as if God were an estate agent.

None of these charges of political ambition can be levelled at the simple men – whether Jewish, Christian or Muslim – who helped to teach us how to live in peace and who were united in one thing: there is only one God and we are all his children.

Another problem that I have tried to resolve, without repudiating what I learned as a child, is the idea of immortality, for my mother believed that when she died she would meet her parents, and my father and brother Michael, and that gave her great comfort. I never tried to dissuade her.

But for me immortality was meaningful in quite a different sense, in that ideas and the spirit survive physical death. As my dad used to say: 'Every life is like a pebble dropped into a pool and the ripples go backwards and forwards for ever, even if we cannot see them.'

I see my parents in my brother David and myself, and I see my wife's influence on my children and grandchildren; and we all feel the influence of teachers throughout history who have shaped our thinking and established the values that we attempt to uphold.

Here, in talking of teachers, I see Jesus the Carpenter of Nazareth as one of the greatest teachers, along with Moses and Mohammed. Christianity, Judaism and Islam are all monotheistic religions, teaching that we are brothers and sisters with a responsibility to each other.

My doubts are about the risen Christ and not about the importance of Jesus. Christians claim to have founded a Church in Jesus's name, and my doubts are about this institution rather than about the teachings he left behind.

In part these doubts were influenced by my visit, while I was an RAF pilot on leave from Egypt, to Jerusalem in 1945. I went to the Church of the Holy Sepulchre and saw the Christian sects fighting over their right to a slice of the area where Christ's body was supposed to have lain, and the stone on the top of the Mount of Olives in which a footprint on a rock was the last place on Earth that Jesus's foot was supposed to have touched before ascending to heaven.

I have the deepest respect for those who believe in the virgin birth, the resurrection and the saints, but they do not help me to understand the world, nor do they point to my duty as to how one should live.

There is no wider theological gap than between those who believe that God created man and those who believe that man invented God. But the ethics of the humanist, the Christian, Jew or Muslim can be so close as to be almost indistinguishable.

I always ask people about their religious faith, and recently a man told me that he was a 'lapsed atheist' who did not believe in God, but had come to believe in the spirituality in all human beings and to respect it and believe that it had a value over and above what science could teach us about the world. I found that very convincing, because we must all try to lead a good life assisted by the prophets of the Old Testament, and Jesus and Mohammed.

Tom Paine said, 'My country is the world and my religion is to do good,' and added, 'We have it in our power to start the world again.' I have evolved from being a devout boy, through doubt and distrust in religious structures, to acceptance of the lessons the great religious teachers have taught.

I hope that my mother would have understood what I am trying to say and that, although my ideas have developed beyond what she taught me, she would recognise the influence she had on my journey of belief.

The role of conscience is a very interesting one: an imbued sense of right or wrong. At any one moment I know what I should do, even if I don't do it; and I know what I shouldn't do, even if

I am doing it. It is a burden, but also a guide to the good life, helping me to see my way through the very complicated questions one has to deal with. It also embodies the idea of accountability. Whether you believe that you are accountable on the Day of Judgement for the way you have spent your life, or have to account to your fellow men and women for what you have done during your life, accountability is a strong and democratic idea.

The next part of this book describes my childhood and growing up within this social and political culture; the third part comprises speeches and essays on some of the moral and political challenges of recent times, reflecting the influence on my life of the dissenting tradition and the need always to question the conventional wisdom of the time.

Part Two

Then

1

Family Tree

The family trait of stubbornness and independence can be traced back at least to my great-grandfather Julius, born in 1826. His father was a master quiltmaker in Manchester, and young Julius ran away from home because of difficulties with his father's second wife; he walked the thirty miles to Liverpool and was found, according to a family autobiography, gazing into the Mersey by a passing Quaker. Urging Julius to follow him, the Quaker acquired lodgings for him and helped him with an education; Julius got a job as a teacher, then he married and at one time ran a boys' 'reformatory' school in Northamptonshire. He later became a non-conformist – Congregational – minister.

On my mother's side there was also a background of religious dissent and, interestingly, both families had a common entrepreneurial spirit and sense of public service.

The two family firms – Eadie Brothers, established by my great-grandfather Peter Eadie, and Benn Brothers, set up by my grandfather John Williams Benn – have both disappeared now, having been absorbed or wound up by bigger units, which saw the

Benn Family Tree

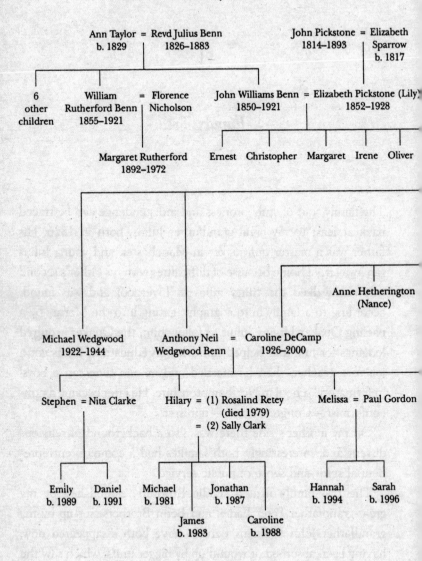

Family Tree

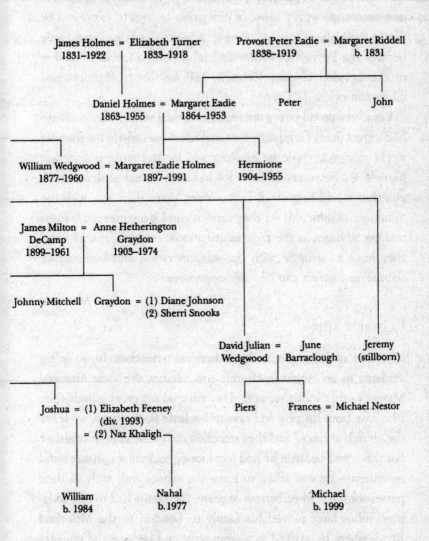

James Holmes = Elizabeth Turner
1831–1922   1833–1918

Provost Peter Eadie = Margaret Riddell
1838–1919   b. 1831

Daniel Holmes = Margaret Eadie
1863–1955   1864–1953

Peter

John

William Wedgwood = Margaret Eadie Holmes
1877–1960   1897–1991

Hermione
1904–1955

James Milton = Anne Hetherington
DeCamp   Graydon
1899–1961   1903–1974

Johnny Mitchell   Graydon = (1) Diane Johnson
                              (2) Sherri Snooks

David Julian = June
Wedgwood   Barraclough

Jeremy
(stillborn)

Joshua = (1) Elizabeth Feeney
              (div. 1993)
       = (2) Naz Khaligh

Piers

Frances = Michael Nestor

William
b. 1984

Nahal
b. 1977

Michael
b. 1999

value of what they did, acquired them and lost the personal touch they embodied. Both firms were typical of Victorian imaginativeness combined with a sense of obligation to society, expressed by the individuals concerned serving in elected office. Peter Eadie became the Provost of Paisley and John Benn a founder member of the London County Council, MP for Tower Hamlets and Chairman of the LCC.

I am very proud of my ancestors and, as a result, I have always had a great deal of sympathy for small businesses where the founder works alongside those he employs and in that sense is a worker himself. As Secretary of State for Industry, I tried to devise policies that would help small businessmen make their way with the minimum of difficulty, for they cannot employ a battery of lawyers and tax advisers, as the huge multinational corporations do – and they have to struggle with the administration and bureaucracy themselves, which can be most oppressive.

FATHER'S SIDE

It is said of Julius Benn that when, as a teacher, he took his students to an Anglican church one Sunday, the vicar attacked Martin Luther in his sermon. This enraged my great-grandfather, who rose from his pew and said to his little flock, 'Boys, we leave the church at once,' and they marched out of the church together. For this – and because he had lost money backing an unsuccessful invention – he was asked to leave the school and, with all their possessions in a wheelbarrow or pram, the family had to find lodgings. Julius later moved his family to London to the Mile End Road, where he worked as a newsagent and became the minister of the Gravel Pit Chapel in Hackney.

One of his children, John Benn (my grandfather), described the 'reduced circumstances' in which they lived. John went to work on his first day as an office boy in the City of London when he was eleven, wearing his mother's pair of 'Sunday boots'. Suffering some of the humiliations that many office boys experience, he wrote about this in his autobiography *The Joys of Adversity*.

John found himself employed by Lawes Randall and Co., a wholesale furniture company in City Road, as a junior invoice clerk. But he had a talent for art and practised drawing, inspired by the draughtsmen and designers, and later became a designer for the firm. By 1880 he had become a junior partner, and this enabled him to establish a little illustrated trade paper of his own, called *The Cabinet Maker*. This struggling business kept him going, despite regular financial difficulties, and he earned extra money later by lecturing, during which he would draw lightning-quick sketches of prominent figures; he also drew sketches of his parliamentary colleagues after he had been elected as a Liberal MP in 1892. At his peak John was earning £2,000 per year from lectures. One of his sketches showed housing in Bethnal Green:

His real love was London and he had a desire to improve the lot of the Londoner. He was a member of the first London County Council, which met in 1889 with a massive 2:1 Progressive majority against the Moderates (Conservatives).

Writing of that occasion, John Benn said, 'The Progressives were already full of great schemes, mostly framed to secure a millennium for London by return of post. The Reformers, fresh from the polls, hotly resented any obstruction to their wishes. They were indeed in deadly earnest.' John was a genuine entrepreneur, combining enterprise with a passionate belief in municipal trading, including the common management and ownership of the tramways, gas, water and electricity. The story of the introduction of electric trams, and Grandfather's role, is most interesting.

The Progressives' strategy was to buy out the many privately owned horse-drawn tram companies, whose operations brought chaos to London's transport system, and to introduce electric trams. Despite stubborn resistance, the first LCC electric trams were inaugurated in May 1903 and ran until 1952. John Benn believed that the revenue from fares could be used to reduce rates and alleviate the 'disgraceful conditions' of the poor; tramway employees received a minimum wage (twenty-five shillings) for a maximum sixty-hour week.

My grandfather fought a notable battle against the 'surface' or 'stud' system for trams, whereby connection was made between the tram and a wire contact in the road. The system was introduced by the Moderates and was supposedly cheaper, but had caused the death of a horse and cars to catch fire, because many of the studs were found to be live. John spoke about 'the terrible story of the Mile End Road from June 24th to July 12th last. Fifty live studs a day injured people, roasted horses, caused fireworks at night and the danger of a fatal accident to any person who chanced to touch a live stud.' The tram company sued my grandfather for libel, and in November 1910 the court assessed damages against him at £12,000. The judge directed that '£5,000 must be secured within 14 days'. An order was put on his property to guarantee payment and, anticipating the bailiffs, my grandmother marked some of the furniture as hers; but my grandfather won on appeal in March 1911. He was congratulated by, among others, a man called Key who wrote, 'I felt as if all the bells ought to be ringing and the flags in the City waving.'

John Benn also advocated leasehold franchisement, the taxation of land values, the abolition of all school fees and public ownership of the Port of London. And he was a strong supporter of women's rights, vigorously defending Lady Sandhurst and two other women who had been chosen by the council as aldermen, but who were disqualified by the courts, because they were women.

John's greatest passion was to secure for Londoners the right to have their own elected government to replace the hotchpotch of boards and vestries, which were as corrupt as they were inefficient. He believed that London, as the greatest city in the world, should be allowed to take over responsibility for the new and sprawling community growing up outside the old City of London, and the City itself under its Lord Mayor and aldermen and livery companies. These enjoyed immense wealth, but had no interest in the people who poured into the City every day to work in the offices and warehouses from which its wealth was derived – and John always believed that its riches should be shared.

As Chairman of the Housing Committee, he was very proud of what the new LCC was able to achieve, acquiring great tracts of land for building. And he campaigned actively to raise the rates of relief in 1893–4 at a time when distress among the poor was at its worst for twenty years.

In 1892 my grandfather had supported John Burns in his campaign for trade-union rates of pay, hours and conditions for contractors to the council. That same year, when the National Telephone Company asked permission to have the streets of London dug up to accommodate its new cable system, the LCC objected, and John led the delegation to see the Postmaster-General to demand that the new telephone service should be seen as a public utility and brought into public ownership.

Arnold Morley, the Postmaster General, refused, saying that the telephone was a luxury. To this my grandfather, showing great foresight, replied that 'The day will come when ordinary people will be able to order their groceries through the telephone.' He lived to see a Liberal government bring the National Telephone Company into the Post Office's own system.

He was equally radical in his attitude to the police, on one occasion calling for an inquiry into the severe injuries sustained, at the hands of the police, by unemployed demonstrators at Tower Hill. And he moved the motion in the council in April 1889 which declared it to be necessary and expedient that the LCC should, in common with all other municipal bodies, have control of its own police. However, London never succeeded in this because Sir William Harcourt, the Home Secretary, argued that the dangers of 'Irish terrorism' necessitated government control.

In 1894 Lord Salisbury denounced the LCC as the place where 'collectivist and socialistic experiments were tried'; the *Daily Mail* included John Benn, along with John Burns and Sidney Webb, on its 'blacklist' in the LCC elections that year.

In 1892 my grandfather had been elected MP for St George'sin-the-East, declaring that he aspired 'to the honour of being a member for the backstreets'. He used this little verse as his slogan:

> Friends of Labour, Working Men
> Stick to Gladstone, Vote for Benn.

John was a passionate believer in Home Rule for Ireland and defeated C. J. Ritchie, who was then President of the Local Government Board, receiving a message of congratulations from Mr Gladstone himself.

After losing his seat in 1895 by eleven votes, having forgotten to vote for himself, he stood in the Deptford by-election in 1897, calling for a bigger house-building programme and for cheap fares for workmen. A scurrilous campaign was mounted against him in a newspaper called *The Sun* owned by Harry Marks, which circulated to every elector a special edition attacking John Benn. He was defeated by 324 votes, a result that led John Burns to announce that 'The election had been won by a newspaper owned by blackguards, edited by scoundrels.' Later, in the General Election of 1900, my grandfather stood for Bermondsey, where he was again defeated. He was ultimately successful in re-entering Parliament for Devonport.

As Chairman also of the LCC, he set out in 1904 his political philosophy in these words, describing the role of the council as guardian of the plain citizen, and foreshadowing the Beveridge Report forty years later:

The Council now follows and guards him from the cradle to the grave. It looks after his health, personal safety and afflicted relatives; it protects him from all sorts of public nuisances; it endeavours to see that he is decently housed or itself houses him.

It keeps an eye on his coal cellar and his larder; it endeavours to make his city more beautiful or convenient; it looks after his municipal purse and corporate property and treasures his historical memories.

It tends and enriches his broad acres and small open spaces and cheers him with music.

It sees that those it employs directly or indirectly enjoy tolerable wages and fair conditions.

It speaks up for him in Parliament, both as to what he wants and what he does not want; and last and greatest of all, it now looks after his children, good and bad, hoping, if it is possible, to make them better and wiser than their progenitors.

In 1910 he spoke alongside Keir Hardie at a rally in Hyde Park in support of Lloyd George's Budget.

One of the last decisions taken by the LCC was to acquire the site on the river on which its home, County Hall, was built. It was Mrs Thatcher who abolished its successor, the Greater London Council, because she did not believe in any of the principles that John Benn espoused.

John was very popular with children and once composed a children's prayer: 'O God, please make the bad people good and the good people nice.' He also wrote 'The Christmas Pudding Song' which I remember my father singing at Christmas, to the tune of 'Sing a Song of Sixpence':

> Once there was a pudding
> At least I fancied so

She had three little children
Whose names I think you know
There was Peter Mincepie first
Michael Orange sitting by
And little Lucy Lemon who
Seemed just about to cry.

Chorus: Sing a song of Pudding full of spice and plums
Crowned with glistening holly, when old Xmas comes
Pass the pudding plates and have another slice
And clap clap clap for Christmas time and everything that's nice.

Worthy Mistress Pudding who had so wise a head
She always gave a raisin for everything she said
She plummed her neighbours up with spicy compliments
Her words were also eatable and with the currant went.
Chorus

Little Peter Mincepie was so cut up one day
He always was so crusty and had a nasty way
Of making very ill the folks who took him in
They couldn't sleep a wink at night he kicked up such a din.
Chorus

Little Michael Orange was such a charming boy
To make his playmates happy was ever Michael's joy
He covered them with juice and though they sucked him dry
This very happy little chap was never known to cry.
Chorus

Little Lucy Lemon whenever she was squeezed
She always pulled a nasty face and said 'I won't be teased'
She always was so cross she never got a kiss
Whatever you do, dear boys and girls, don't get a face
  like this.

John Benn died in 1922, three years before I was born, and I am very sad never to have met him. As I have got older, I have come to appreciate what a tremendously progressive force local government has been in the history of our democracy. Had the Labour Party existed when he was first elected, he would certainly have been a member of it. He was a passionate advocate of what came to be known as 'gas-and-water socialism', which laid the foundations of the welfare state. After his death his son, my Uncle Ernest, opened the John Benn Hostel for homeless boys in the East End in memory of his father.

In 1958, when my dad was just over eighty, he did a broadcast for the BBC and his opening words were, 'The chief interest of my family for four generations has been Parliament.' He described how his grandfather, the Revd Julius Benn, had nominated James Bryce as the Liberal candidate for Tower Hamlets; how his father John had been elected for the same constituency in 1892, and he himself for Tower Hamlets in 1906. His broadcast ended by describing how my two eldest sons had sat in the gallery of the House of Lords waving to him, knowing that their father, their grandfather and both their great-grandfathers had been Members of Parliament. And he ended, 'You will understand then what I mean when I speak of a parliamentary community and why I live so happy in a blaze of autumn sunshine.'

My dad could not know then that one of those little boys (my son Hilary) would himself become an MP for Leeds and is now a Cabinet minister, helping to make a record of five members of the family over four generations in Parliament in three centuries.

MOTHER'S SIDE

On my mother's side my Scottish ancestors were radical in nature, and it is said that my great-great-grandmother was in Stirling on the day of the execution of two Scots radicals – John Baird and Andrew Hardie – for armed insurrection in 1820.

My great-grandfather on Mother's side was Peter Eadie, a Scots engineer who was apprenticed on the Clyde. The Eadies were farmers in Perthshire, but Peter travelled widely in Europe, as many Scottish engineers did in the nineteenth century, and was involved in building the railway station at Kilmarnock.

Peter Eadie was a very imaginative man. He invented a device called a Ring Traveller, which was a modest invention that was essential for the textile industry. And in his little house in Galashiels he designed and manufactured these tiny components, set up a small company and then moved to Paisley, a textile centre. There he built up a very successful business with two brothers (the company being called Eadie Bros and Co.) with £120 capital.

Politically he was a radical on Paisley council and disliked the 'idle rich' intensely. My mother said that the first time she heard the word 'socialist' was after the election of the Liberal government in 1906, when Peter declared that he might go further than them and 'become a socialist'. In his capacity as a

Paisley councillor, he supported votes for women and in 1913 wrote:

> I will give my blessing to anyone who will bring in a measure to redress her [woman's] wrongs. Of course I do not know all the circumlocutions of the House of Commons nor how long it would take them to do it, but if they would hand it over to the Paisley Town Council they would do the job at a sitting.

Peter Eadie's daughter, my maternal grandmother, Margaret, who worked on the Ring Traveller in Galashiels, met and married Daniel Holmes, who was born in 1863, the son of a steeplejack in Irvine. Daniel was a brilliant student who had become a teacher at Paisley Grammar School, having come first in the external examination for a degree at London University. The Holmes family belonged to the Irvine Brethren, a strict Christian sect.

Daniel also travelled up and down Scotland giving lectures at public libraries that had been funded by James Coats, a wealthy Scots industrialist. He wrote a book about it called *Literary Tours in the Highlands and Islands of Scotland*, which gives a vivid account of his travels and the very intellectual attitude of the Scots, together with their readiness to engage in intense discussions about political and theological questions.

He was very absent-minded. Mother told us that after leaving school he had been unsuccessfully apprenticed to a tailor. He was sent round to take the measurements of the customers, who later refused to accept the finished suits because they were all wrong. When Daniel and my grandmother went cycling on their honeymoon, she had a puncture and he cycled on, waving cheerily and saying, 'I'll see you back at the hotel', leaving his bride to walk back alone.

Although when I knew Daniel, in old age, he seemed very conservative in his outlook and his liberalism appeared to me to be far to the right, he was reported – when adopted as a parliamentary candidate for Govan – as saying, 'I am a radical by conviction, I shall give my utmost support to any measure which, in my opinion, is for the social wellbeing of the people. One great reason for our social misery is that too much of the land in this country is in the hands of private individuals.' In these opinions he may well have been influenced by his father-in-law, Peter Eadie, who was a genuine radical.

In 1911 Daniel was duly elected to Parliament for Govan (in a by-election), and Mother told me that his political meetings were very well attended because he would use them to explore and explain his knowledge of ancient history. On one occasion he described to an interested audience that just before Vesuvius erupted, there was an election in Pompeii; he held his audience in rapt attention, although it had little to do with the manifesto on which he was standing.

He made his maiden speech on the Temperance (Scotland) Bill and entranced the House by saying, 'I do not expect that, in our generation at least, alcohol will ever be out of date and when I look at the history and even the climate of my native country I know quite well that my fellow countrymen will never be sickeningly abstemious or ostentatiously teetotal.'

He was a talented poet and became known as the Poet Laureate of the House of Commons. One poem, which I quoted at my own retirement party in the Speaker's House in 2001, ran as follows:

> Though politicians dream of fame
> And hope to win a deathless name

Time strews upon them when they've gone
The poppy of oblivion.
But lo the singer and his lays
Grow mightier with the lapse of days
And soar above the wreck of time
On the immortal wings of rhyme.

Daniel Holmes was not really a politician, but a teacher, and in that capacity he represented perfectly the deep commitment of his fellow countrymen and women to education and the importance of learning – describing himself as 'a worshipper at learning's shrine'. He was scholarly to the end and always carried around a copy of Dante's *Inferno* in his pocket, and suitcases full of books.

I knew both my grandparents on my mother's side, as they lived into the 1950s. But Mother had a strange childhood, because Daniel, being a very old-fashioned Scottish teacher, took little interest in her education and she spent much time in France and Switzerland as a child, because her parents moved there for a time; she learned French there, and was educated at home, though by the age of seven or eight she had not been taught to read or write properly. She never went to university, but compensated for this by developing her own interest in theology and studied for an STh (Student of Theology) qualification at King's College London, after she had married my father and while she was having her children.

I had many interesting aunts, uncles and cousins, of whom two stand out in my memory.

My Uncle Ernest

My father and his elder brother were both Liberals, but whereas Ernest was a 'Manchester School' Liberal, Father was a radical Liberal, and Ernest was very upset when Father decided in 1927 to join the Labour Party. But Father had a great deal of respect and affection for Ernest's kindness towards our family.

We used to spend Christmas at his house in Oxted, Surrey – Blunt House – during my childhood up until 1935. Ernest was married to Gwen, who somewhat disapproved of my father. She was a magistrate and my father who, as a Privy Counsellor, could sit in any magistrate's court, would tease her, threatening to come and sit in hers.

Ernest was a very good businessman; he took over the struggling trade-publications company Benn Brothers, founded by his father John, and turned it into a thriving business. After the First World War, Ernest had decided to move into book publishing and set up a new company called Ernest Benn, which was a great success, so that by 1918 he was earning £10,000 a year. This is why he was able to buy his grand Surrey mansion. Ernest was also extremely careful with money.

A young man called Victor Gollancz had been working voluntarily in my father's parliamentary office, but decided that politics was not his interest, so Father suggested that he might go into publishing and recommended him to Ernest. Long before the advent of Penguin Books, Ernest introduced Benn's Sixpenny Novels and they were a tremendous success, largely due to Victor; but when Victor asked my uncle to make him a partner, on the basis of the contribution he had made, Ernest refused. And so Gollancz left the firm and established his own publishing house.

Gollancz Books became an even greater success, and among the many titles for which Victor became famous were the Left Book Club publications, which had a profound impact on the development of socialist ideas during the 1930s. I once had the pleasure of hearing Gollancz speak during the war in a debate in Oxford about the need to admit Jewish refugees to Britain; it was so powerful that the students voted unanimously in favour of the motion.

Ernest was also a very successful writer and his most famous book, *The Confessions of a Capitalist*, sold hundreds of thousands of copies and was published worldwide. He was an unashamed advocate of market forces, like Margaret Thatcher years later – whose election would have delighted him, although Ernest would have been very doubtful about the idea that a woman should have the responsibility of being Prime Minister. Ernest wrote another book about Russia, which began with the clear and simple statement that he had never been to Russia and had no intention of doing so while the Soviet regime continued to exist.

He engaged in public debates with Jimmy Maxton, the Scottish socialist; founded the Society of Individualists and, on principle, refused when he was in his seventies to fill in his census form for 1951, on the grounds that it was an infringement of his right to privacy. He was taken to court, and his barrister – in an attempt to be helpful – said, 'I hope Your Honour will take account of the fact that Sir Ernest Benn is a very old man.' This infuriated my uncle, who sacked his lawyer on the spot, pleaded guilty and was duly fined, but retained his self-respect.

Like Margaret Thatcher, Ernest was a genuine libertarian on

Great grandfather, the Rev. Julius Benn, minister of the Gravel Pit Chapel, Hackney, murdered by his son, William, during a bout of insanity

Laying the tracks for the LCC's electric trams on Victoria Embankment.

Grandfather John Benn, as Chairman of the LCC, reviews the London Fire Brigade, with its horse-drawn engines in 1904.

John Benn, 1904
(painted by Sir William Orpen).

Father, then Secretary of State for Air, in
Alexandria, 1946, during the negotiations for a
revision of the 1936 Anglo-Egyptian Treaty.

Great grandfather Peter Eadie
as Provost of Paisley, 1905.

I met David Lloyd George in 1937 knowing that
Father didn't trust him and had left the Liberal
Party when Lloyd George became leader.

Grandfather Holmes, a teacher at Paisley
Grammar School, who became MP for Govan.

Mother, as the first President, inaugurates the Congregational Federation, London, 1972.

Father (left) and Grandfather Holmes (top hat) on the terrace of the House of Commons, 1913.

The family home, 40 Grosvenor Road, later renamed 40 Millbank, where I was born. Sidney and Beatrice Webb lived next door and both houses were demolished to make way for Millbank Tower: Clause 4 of the Labour Party constitution was drafted (by the Webbs) and repealed (by New Labour) on the very same site.

Benn Brothers, Ernest and William, by the seaside, 1926.

Stansgate then (1899)...

...and now (2004)

Michael's 8th birthday: with the family on the beach at Stansgate, 1929, in front of the old Coastguard Hut.

My cousin, Margaret Rutherford: she made the part of Madame Arcati in *Blithe Spirit* her own.

David, aged 8, in his busman's uniform talking to
a fellow driver at Victoria Station, 1936.

Me leaving for Gladstone's
School, aged 11.

Oswald 'Tom' Mosley.
I saw Mosley twice: once
in 1928 when he was a
Labour MP and seven
years later as the leader
of the British Union of
Fascists marching near
Parliament Square.

As a keen member of the 52nd Westminster
Troop. (*Left*) Scout Camp, Isle of Mull, 1939.

Nurse Olive Winch caring for David
during his convalescence, March 1938.
(*Right*) Grandfather and Grandmother
Holmes with David who was
convalescing at Bexhill

Standing for Parliament,
Victoria Tower Garden,
June 1931.

Me, aged 7, checkmating
Uncle Ernest, 58, in the
garden of Blunt House.

The Ragamuffins,
Stansgate, Summer 1932
(Father behind David).

Mother with her 'boys'
preparing for a sail on
the River Blackwater,
Essex, Summer 1934.

Mum and Dad at Stansgate, just before war was declared, August, 1939.

Olive Winch with Michael, 18, David, 11 and me, with Father sitting on the steps at Stansgate.

On active service: the family in London during the Blitz, 1940.

On May 10, 1941, 550 German bombers blasted London. Much of Westminster, including the school and House of Commons, was damaged or destroyed.

The last photograph taken of all the family together; Mike died on operations seven months later.

the right in British politics. By contrast my father, who was also a Gladstonian Liberal, had acquired from the Grand Old Man a passion for liberty, which made him a rebel against the authority that money claimed to have over individuals. When he joined the Labour Party, Father moved naturally to the left – much like the Foot family, of which Michael (and later Dingle) found his natural home in the Labour Party, along with Josiah (Josh) Wedgwood, who joined the Labour Party on the same day as my dad in 1926.

It is assumed that I am related to the Wedgwoods. I always understood that my grandfather, who was an artist and greatly admired the work of the potter, gave the name Wedgwood to my father as a second Christian name, and my father did the same with all his children. My mother used to say that she thought that one of the family may have married a Wedgwood in the nine-teenth century.

Relations between Uncle Ernest and his brother Will, my father, were rather complex. Ernest was generous to my father, who had worked as a journalist on Benn Brothers trade magazines and continued to receive assistance from him while an MP until salaries of £400 a year were introduced in 1910. Ernest also helped Father when he returned from the war in 1918 and lost his seat, due to boundary redistribution, and had to find a new constituency elsewhere; and lent him £1,500 to buy Stansgate, a retreat and holiday home in Essex, at a time when he was out of Parliament. Uncle Ernest generously allowed me to work for Benn Brothers after leaving Oxford, which meant that I could travel to America in 1949, ostensibly on behalf of the company, but with the real purpose of visiting my future wife, Caroline.

When I returned to Britain in 1949, Ernest was not prepared

to re-engage me, which was why I was lucky to get my first paid job as a BBC producer at the princely salary of £9 a week.

MARGARET RUTHERFORD

It was through visiting my Uncle Ernest that I met my cousins, who were all much older than me, because Father was forty-three when he married. My first cousin once removed, the actress Margaret Rutherford, was my father's first cousin.

She used to come to Blunt House for Christmas and seemed to me to be quite old, though she was only in her early forties and was making a living as a teacher of elocution and doing repertory theatre, hoping to make it big on the stage.

Many young girls want to go onstage, but it is unusual for that desire to be so strong later in life, and we used to treat this as an eccentricity. To the surprise and delight of the whole family, Margaret became a superstar, appearing in Noel Coward's play *Spring Meeting* in 1933 and until her death in 1972 moving from triumph to triumph, one of her most successful performances being as Madame Arcati in *Blithe Spirit*, and playing a medieval historian in *Passport to Pimlico*. She also appeared with Alastair Sim in another famous film, *The Happiest Days of Your Life*, in which a girls' and a boys' school found themselves sharing the same premises during the war, and she and the boys' headmaster were drawn into a conspiracy to prevent the parents from discovering this fact.

We had another sweet great-aunt called Auntie Tweenie, who lived in Oxted in a tiny house, which I think my uncle had bought for her and where we had tea on Boxing Day with cakes that she had baked; Margaret Rutherford watched her carefully and affectionately and I have an idea that some of her stage characters were based on her observations.

What I did not know at the time, and only discovered by chance later, was the family tragedy that lay behind Margaret's story. I had often wondered how Margaret Rutherford was related to us and, if she was, why her surname was not Benn. When I asked about her father I was always brushed aside. If I tried to press my mother, all she would say was, 'Darling, he never did anything to be ashamed of.' And it was only when I was a Member of Parliament that I decided to consult *The Times* index and found the headline in 1883 about Margaret's father, who murdered his own father, Julius.

Margaret's father was William Rutherford Benn, son of Julius Benn (my great-grandfather). William married Florence Nicholson in 1883, but had some sort of a mental breakdown on his honeymoon and spent a short spell in an asylum. Then his father, Julius, decided to take William on holiday to Matlock in Derbyshire to help him recover. While they were there, William killed Julius with a chamberpot in the lodgings they had taken in the town, and then tried to cut his own throat; he lived and was found, next to the body of his dead father, by the police.

William Rutherford Benn was sent to Broadmoor and to this day I do not know whether Margaret Rutherford ever knew what had happened to her father. Later he began to recover and the Home Secretary at the time released him. Margaret was born some time after this sad saga.

William later went to India as a journalist, but when his brother John heard that he had decided to remarry there following the death of Florence, he felt obliged to stop the marriage. When William returned to England, he was recommitted. William was my father's favourite uncle, and the tragedy had a profound effect on his life.

When my dad was about to marry my mother in 1920, my grandfather John actually wrote to my mother's father to report this history, though it never occurred to him to write direct to my mother, who was, after all, the bride about to marry into a family with this tragic background. This absolutely incensed Mother's mother, who came out against the wedding and stood outside the church while the marriage took place, announcing to all and sundry that she was not in favour of it; it is not clear to me whether the guests of the wedding in St Margaret's Church in Westminster knew who this strange lady was.

Margaret Rutherford herself later married an actor called Stringer Davis, and it was part of an understanding that he would always have a small role in the films in which she was taking part.

Margaret was always very kind to me, and I have many happy memories of sitting with her on the beach at Bexhill as a child, and of occasions when we met in the years before her death.

The *News of the World* once paid a genealogist to research the Benn ancestry. It discovered the story and printed photographs of Margaret and of me, to imply that I had a streak of inherited madness. I worried what political damage this might do, but the only reference ever made to me about it was from a friendly London cab driver, who said, 'I am sorry to hear about your uncle!' So much for the power of the press.

2

My Parents

Unfortunately for the reader, I cannot claim a tragic childhood, rebellion against parents or a struggle to make a success of life from hard beginnings, for I had a happy home and my parents were devoted to each other, and at no time did I react against what I was taught by them. Everything rotated around Father, in a way that would be unacceptable today, and this was a pattern which to some extent I followed – to my regret in later life.

FATHER

My dad was a Victorian, born in 1877 and in many ways practising what we think of as Victorian values: very conscious of the need never to waste time or money. I was born in 1925, and as a child I was required to keep an account book showing how I had spent my pocket money each week, which then had to be audited by my father's secretary, Miss Triggs, before my next pocket money was paid.

63

Accounts
Started
21st Oct 1934 age 9½

Dear dad
I happily and
heartily start hoping them
to be a great Success and
I agree in every to the rules
micheal agreed to and alsoed
the longer was I nought
3d p.m.
yours
succeddfully
A. N. W. Benn

Oct 1934

accounts anew

My accounts
have so far
been unsuccess-
ful but it is
never toolate to
start anew
is it? I may
have many falls
before
perfection but
as it is my
attempt it is
probable it
will be near
my if not
lost
a. n. u. Benn

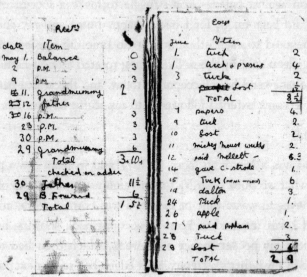

Rec'd		
date	Item	
may 1.	Balance	0
2	P.M.	3
9	P.M.	3
11	Grandmummy	2
12	father	1
16	P.M.	3
23	P.M.	3
30	P.M.	3
29	Grandmummy	6
	Total	3.10s
	checked on adder	
30	Father	11½
29	B Forward	6
	Total	1 5½

Exp		
June	Item	
1.	tuck	2
1	Arch's present	4
3	tuck	2
.	lost	½
	TOTAL	8½
7	papers	4.
9	tuck	2.
10	lost	2.
11	mickey mouse weekly	2.
12	paid mellett	6.3
14	gave c-strode	1.
15	tuck (none missed)	6
19	dalton	3.
24	tuck	1.
26	apple	1.
27	paid potham	2.
28	tuck	3
28	lost	2
	TOTAL	2 9

I received one penny a week, rising to tuppence when I went to school, and made up to threepence if I submitted my accounts promptly. I recall on one occasion when I was taking an early interest in carpentry, I went to Woolworths and bought a little vice and Miss Triggs queried this – though what vice an eight-year-old could have paid for was beyond my imagination.

Father used to call out 'Antonio' if he wanted me to do something. He referred to me as a 'serving brother' because I was a very helpful boy, always keen to be popular, cycling to the village to post letters, buy papers and so on, and on one occasion I said to him, 'I want our relations to be on a strictly business-like basis.' So when I was sent to the village near Stansgate to post a letter, I told him, 'That will be a shilling.' Father replied, 'And your lunch costs two shillings and sixpence.' So that was the end of that!

My elder brother Michael and I would set up little businesses. We had one that made cigarettes (Jigarettes, as my father called them, because my nickname was Jiggs) using a roller and cigarette papers. Michael was very inventive, and there was a model aeroplane at that time called a 'Frog', powered by an elastic band that set the propeller off. He worked out that it would be possible to have two elastic bands working consecutively, thus doubling the range of the Frog. He took it to the company that produced the Frog, which was interested and gave Michael a model to experiment with.

Phone calls were regarded as totally unnecessary luxuries, and I can remember many occasions when, having asked permission from my dad to use the phone, he would say, 'Why don't you send a postcard?' At Stansgate, where we had a house for summer holidays, he had a call box attached to the phone, which we had to feed with coins before we could use it; although my father had a key to the cash box, we still had to cycle to the village of Steeple nearby to get change if we wanted to make a call. Occasionally the electricity (also on a cash meter) would run out while Sunday lunch was cooking; this happened many years later when my wife Caroline was trying to produce a meal at Stansgate.

Father's passion for economy was matched by an equally strict view of the importance of not wasting time, since he had read a book published by Arnold Bennett in 1908 called *How to Live on Twenty-four Hours a Day*. Bennett's argument was that we are all equal in one respect, namely that no one has more than twenty-four hours in a day and no one has less, and that we each have a moral responsibility to make full use of the time allocated to us. For this reason Father kept a daily time chart on which he set down the number of hours he worked every day and the number of hours that he slept; in theory it should equal twenty-four – a curious calculation in that there was no time for meals, conversation or any social life. So keen was he on this that, as a boy, I was expected to keep a time chart. I still have one in my own archives (see opposite page), which no doubt explains why the wise use of time has been a major factor in shaping my thinking, making me feel guilty – even to this day – if I go to bed believing that I have achieved nothing. My house has always been full of clocks. Father never went on 'holiday' and his answer to depression was overwork.

Regular bowel movements were considered very important, and Father, though he took absolutely no interest in our domestic routine, would unfailingly enquire every day, 'Have you caught the bus yet?' – a euphemism that I have never heard used elsewhere for this particular function.

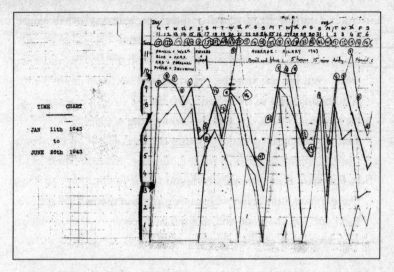

Father was a teetotaller because, having been born in the East End of London (which he loved), he had been much stirred by the problem of drunkenness there. His parents were keen members of the Blue Ribbon Brigade, active campaigners for temperance. At the time, drink was seen as a problem, rather like that of drugs today, contributing to the destruction of many lives; gin, at a penny a pint, was described as 'mother's ruin'.

Father once said that his parents used to sing temperance hymns, one of which began with the words, 'There's a serpent in the glass, dash it down, dash it down'. Another also had a splendid double-entendre: 'The good ship temperance is heading for the port.' He used to recite the story of 'Timothy Prout', who fancied a night out and, when he returned home to Fulham, entered the wrong house and was found fast asleep by the real owner. Timothy swore he would never have another drink. The story was also a reference, I think, to new housing at the time, because the villa in which Timothy lived had the same key as every other house in the street.

> Let me tell you the story of Timothy Prout
> Who had fancied to live a little way out
> He was tired of the dirt and the din and the noise
> And the rudeness of so many young city boys.
>
> In Fulham a neat little villa he found
> Quite a nice little house with its own piece of ground
> Each one was the same and as any could see
> The front doors all used the very same key.
>
> One night when he'd had just a bit much to drink
> He wandered back home quite unable to think
> But he soon saw his house and opened the door
> And dropped all his things and sank down to the floor.
>
> Then in came a woman who gave a big scream
> And Timothy woke up as if from a dream
> Then her husband came in and with just a small frown
> Said, 'Oh yes sir, I've frequently met you in town.'
>
> As Timothy rose from his place on the floor
> The man said, 'You'll find your own house next door'
> So Timothy left and resolved without doubt
> That he never again would mix gin with his stout.

Father asked me not to drink alcohol and I never have done so, although when I joined the RAF in 1942 he gave me his permission to do what I thought right. But long ago I decided to keep alcohol for my old age, which today seems as far away as ever.

I suppose my grandparents were puritanical in outlook, but I hope I have not given the impression that my father was a severe man, for he was full of fun and the jokes he made remain with me to this day and often come to mind. Mother was nervous of bats, and Father once tied some string to a piece of coal and swung it from the ceiling in a dark bedroom. He used to amuse the children of his sister-in-law, my Aunt Gwen, with stories about a pink giraffe, which Gwen thought silly and disapproved of. So Father said, 'All right, the pink giraffe will die.' And he then proceeded to tell long stories about the pink giraffe's funeral. He was everyone's favourite uncle. He would recite a poem about the Lord Mayor's coachman, who promised to get the Lord Mayor from Mansion House in the City of London to Buckingham Palace, without going down any streets:

The Lord Mayor had a coachman
The coachman's name was John
Said the Lord Mayor to the coachman:
'Take your wages and begone
I want a better coachman
For I am going to see the Queen.'
Said John: 'I am the finest coachman,
That was ever seen
And if you'll let me drive today
I'll show I can't be beat
I'll drive to Buckingham Palace and

49

I won't go thro' a street.'
'You must be mad,' the Lord Mayor said,
'But still I'll humour you.
But remember that you lose your place
The first street you go through.'
The coachman jumped upon his box
And settled in his seat;
And started up the Poultry
Which we know's not called a street.
Along Cheapside he gaily went.
The Bobbies cleared the course
To the statue of the Bobby
Who first organised the force.
'You're going into Newgate Street,'
The Lord Mayor loudly bawls.
But John said: 'Tuck your tuppenny in
I'm going round St Paul's.'
'But round St Paul's means Ludgate Hill
And Fleet Street, John,' said he.
But John said: 'I don't go that way
But down the Old Bailey.'
Up Holborn and High Holborn
And St Martin's Lane he drives
And thus to keep out of a street
He artfully contrives
And when they reach Trafalgar Square
Said the Lord Mayor in a pet:
'O dash my wig and barnacles
I think he'll do it yet!'
John nearly drove into the Strand

Then stopped as if in doubt.
'I'm not surprised,'
The Lord Mayor cries
'To find you're put out.
Up Parliament Street you must go
Or else cross Cockspur Street
It's very hard but still
You must admit defeat.'
But John said: 'Not at all, my lord
I don't much think I shall.
You ask me where I'm going:
Well, I'm going down Pall Mall.'
Along Pall Mall he gaily drove
And drove at racing rate
By James's Palace through the Mall
To Buckingham Palace straight.
The coachman gave the Lord Mayor
The Lord Mayor
The Lord Mayor
The coachman gave the Lord Mayor
A curious kind of treat

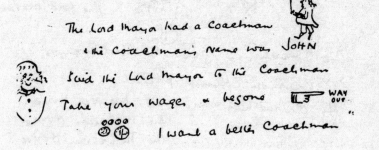

For I'm going to see the Queen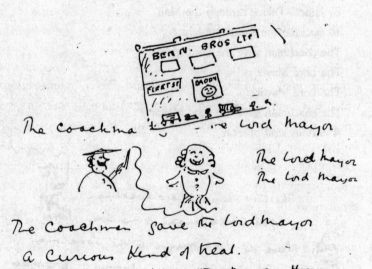

Said John "I am the finest
    Coachman that was ever seen"

And if you'll let me drive today
I'll show I cant be beat
I'll drive to Buckingham Palace
And I won't go
thro a Steel:

"You must be mad" the Lord Mayor
Said "But still I'll humour you

The Coachman gave the Lord Mayor

The Lord Mayor
The Lord Mayor

The Coachman gave the Lord Mayor
A curious kind of treat.
He drove him from the Mansion House
                    the Mansion House
                    the Mansion House

The Mansion House & Buckingham Palace

and

DIDNT GO THROUGH A STREET

He drove him from the Mansion House
The Mansion House
The Mansion House
The Mansion House to Buckingham Palace
And didn't go through a street.

Father once said to me, 'Never wrestle with a chimneysweep', which was a curious piece of advice to give an eight-year-old, but I now understand exactly what he meant: 'If someone plays dirty with you, don't play dirty with him or you will get dirty, too.' My attempt to keep personal abuse out of political controversy has been shaped by that simple phrase about how to steer clear of chimneysweeps. I recommend it to others without reservation.

Father had inherited a distrust of established authority and the conventional wisdom of the powerful, and his passion for freedom of conscience and his belief in liberty explain all the causes he took up during his life, beginning with his strong opposition to the Boer War as a student at University College London, for which he was, on one occasion, thrown out of a ground-floor window by patriotic contemporaries.

He had been sent to France with his brother Ernest in the 1880s and learned to speak French fluently. When he wore a beret, he looked very Gallic. He studied French at university and, after leaving with a first-class honours degree, lived in East London and worked as a journalist for *The Cabinet Maker*, the journal founded by his father, which later became part of Benn Brothers' publishing concern.

By the turn of the century Father was already active in Liberal politics in St George's constituency in Wapping, helping to raise funds for cigar workers locked out in their industrial dispute. He won the unanimous support of the Municipal Employees Union and of Stepney Labour Council when he was adopted as a Liberal parliamentary candidate for Tower Hamlets.

In his 1906 election address he criticised the Tories for 'having made laws for the benefit of their privileged friends and entirely neglected the claims of the workers'. He pledged himself to support legislation 'to protect the funds of trade unions, to support Irish Home Rule and to work for the establishment of a national home for the Jews', helping Jewish refugees who had fled to East London from the pogroms in Tsarist Russia at the end of the nineteenth

century. He made his maiden speech in the House of Commons arguing for the municipal ownership of the Port of London, drawing attention to the rising unemployment among dock workers.

After serving as a Parliamentary Private Secretary (PPS) to Reginald McKenna, the First Lord of the Admiralty, in 1908, Father was made junior Whip in 1910 and carried the responsibility for answering questions in the Commons for the Office of Works, because the First Commissioner of Works, Earl Beauchamp, was in the House of Lords.

In 1914 he volunteered for the Middlesex Yeomanry, although both his age (then thirty-seven) and his membership of the House of Commons would have exempted him from military service. For the next four years he served in the forces fighting at Gallipoli, flying as an observer in sea planes from a passenger ship, the *Ben-My-Chree*, which had been converted into an elementary aircraft carrier. When the *Ben-My-Chree* was sunk by Turkish gunfire, he commanded a small Anglo-French force, holding out in Castellorizo. Later, aged almost forty, he qualified as a pilot and served on the Italian front, where he flew on the night mission with Tandura, the first spy ever dropped by parachute behind enemy lines in Italy.

He once described how he took a saw and cut a hole in the bottom of the plane so that Tandura, the Italian chosen for this operation, could be launched with his parachute and a box of pigeons – being released at an agreed moment when Father pulled the lever that allowed him to fall out of the plane.

Tandura undertook this immensely dangerous task, landed safely and reported on enemy positions by scribbling them on little notes, which he tied to the legs of the carrier pigeons, which then flew back to Headquarters with their important intelligence informa-

May 29, 1912.] PUNCH, OR THE LONDON CHARIVARI. 413

ESSENCE OF PARLIAMENT.
Extracted from the Diary of Toby, M.P.

"YOUTH AT THE PROW AND (MIXED) PLEASURE AT THE HELM."
Mr. F. D. Acland. Mr. Wedgwood Benn. Mr. Asquith.
Sir John Simon. Mr. Herbert Samuel.

A *Punch* cartoon showing Father and some young Radicals with an anxious Prime Minister. *Punch* wrote:

House of Commons, Monday, May 20: To-day we have with us only one BENN, upon whom his godfathers and godmother in his baptism, with prophetic foresight of what in due time would become a precious antique ware, bestowed the name of WEDGWOOD. The twentieth-century LITTLE BENN ranks in Ministry as Junior Lord of Treasury, his place being in the Whips' room or the lobby. PREMIER'S quick eye discerning his capacity, he has this session provided for him a seat on Treasury Bench, where he represents FIRST COMMISSIONER OF WORKS, throned in the Lords.

tion. Tandura survived, and after the war named his own son Wedgwood Benn Tandura. I have often thought of an ageing Italian who must have asked himself why he had such a ridiculous name.

Father was awarded the DSO and the DFC, the Légion d'honneur, the Croix de Guerre and an Italian decoration which he called the 'Fatiguera di Guerra' and translated as 'Sick of the War'.

For him, public service in wartime meant military service and he refused two invitations from Lloyd George (who, by December 1916, had become Prime Minister) to join the government, first as a Parliamentary Secretary and later as joint Chief Whip in the wartime government.

Father's wartime service helped to develop his political philosophy, and his book *In the Sideshows*, about those years in the services, throws some light on it. He saw the old professional army officer as being incapable of 'appreciating the diversities of human character and capacity' and as discouraging 'initiative and energy through class prejudice determined to entrench itself'.

He wrote, 'There are no regulations to say that none but the privileged class is permitted to enter; the existence of class barriers is denied; but those who have been on the inside know perfectly well that the gate is strictly kept.' And he noted the 'inevitable ignorance' of officers who 'live in narrow grooves and are forbidden by the rules of the game to receive any education from those who alone can educate them, namely their subordinates'. 'Wars are peoples in arms,' he argued:

Leaders are needed, military as well as political, who see the difference between a just and an unjust cause; who understand how much ideals count as a practical force, even in the behaviour of individual soldiers; who know that Right is the steam which drives the engine Might.

His experience also made him into an internationalist. It was the war that drove him on to promote international understanding.

On his return home in 1918, he discovered that his constituency had been redistributed and another Liberal candidate was in place. Rather than fight it out, Father accepted a nomination as an independent Liberal for Leith, in opposition to Lloyd George's coalition, and was elected. The next eight years were ones of vigorous parliamentary activity with the Radical group that he jointly led, and it was during those years that he developed his skill as a debater and his reputation as a parliamentarian. He was bitterly opposed to the government's Irish policy and to the use of the 'Black and Tans' against the Irish Nationalists.

In 1920 he moved an amendment in Parliament to the King's Speech, condemning the Coalition for having handed over 'to the military authorities an unrestricted discretion in the definition and punishment of offences' and 'having frustrated the prospects of an agreed settlement of the problems of Irish self-government'. Though he had, earlier, been more attracted to Lloyd George's radical reforms than to Asquith's Whiggery, he deeply mistrusted Lloyd George as a person and detested his coalition with the Tories.

Finding himself voting more and more often with Labour MPs in the Commons, Father finally resigned from the Liberals in 1927 after Lloyd George was elected their leader. He joined the Labour Party, sat for a moment on the Labour benches and applied for the Chiltern Hundreds on the same day – a device used to effect an immediate resignation from Parliament. He thought it right to resign his seat because his constituents had elected him as a Liberal and he believed it was immoral to remain as a Labour MP, a precedent that few who have changed their party allegiance since have followed.

When he and Mother were visiting Moscow in 1926, they witnessed the trade unions marching with their banners in the May Day Parade. He loved to tell us how when he asked an interpreter to translate one of the revolutionary slogans, the answer was: 'Workers of the Electrical Trades improve your qualifications'!

Though Father neither embraced the full socialist economic analysis nor was rooted in the trade unions, he greatly valued the fellowship that his membership of the Labour Party brought him and shared its seriousness of purpose. After attending his first Labour Party Conference in 1927, he wrote in the *Daily Herald* that 'a great sense of responsibility seemed to overshadow the gathering . . . they were making decisions that in the near future would pass from being the resolutions of a Party to becoming the policy of the British government'. Until the end of his life his sympathies remained instinctively with the non-conformists within the Party, especially when attempts were made to impose Party discipline on them, being something of a lone crusader himself.

In 1928 there was a by-election in North Aberdeen and my dad was elected as a Labour MP and a year later was put in the Cabinet in Ramsay MacDonald's second minority government, as Secretary of State for India. It was his first experience as a departmental minister and he had to defend himself in the Commons. Lloyd George, mocking Father's short height, once taunted him as a 'pocket edition of Moses', to which he replied, 'At least I do not worship the golden calf' – a reference to the fact that Lloyd George had sold peerages to boost his own political funds.

Working towards 'Dominion status' for India, he came under heavy attack both from Churchill, the old imperialist who opposed the very idea of Indian independence, and from the Left, who believed that this policy was too slow, and disapproved of Gandhi's imprisonment. But Father did succeed in calling two Round Table conferences and in bringing Gandhi to London as a delegate to the second one.

By the time it was held, however, the Labour government had fallen. In August 1931 Ramsay MacDonald had capitulated to financial pressures and had formed a National government. An interesting insight into MacDonald's mind is given in a letter sent to Labour MPs dated 25 August 1931, justifying the cutting of benefit to unemployed workers, and saying:

> . . . To restore the necessary confidence, as every one of us recognises, it is necessary to balance the Budget, and the problem is how to spread the burden involved equally throughout the community . . . During the past weeks events moved so rapidly that widespread consultation was impossible but I hope you will suspend judgement until the situation has been made clear to you and the facts put in your possession.
>
> All this has caused us great pain. When it is over the Party will be left untrammelled as to its policy and programme . . .

Within three days of that letter MacDonald had been ousted as leader of the Party and a General Election followed, on 28 October 1931.

Father, who fought North Aberdeen on the basis of 'the manifest failure of the outworn creed of "every man for himself"' and called for the establishment of a 'new Social Order', was defeated at the election by the Conservative candidate and found himself out of Parliament again, leaving only fifty Labour MPs in the new House of Commons.

It is easy to forget that, before the calamity of 1931, Ramsay MacDonald had been tremendously successful in building up the Labour Party. He opposed the First World War, and my mother told me that on 4 August 1918 (the anniversary of the outbreak of that war) he came home with my grandfather, Daniel Holmes, because he feared he might be attacked in the street on account of his outspoken opposition to the war.

For five years following the election, Father and Mother travelled very widely, meeting world leaders and writing about it together in a book entitled *Beckoning Horizon*, which dealt with the politics and religious beliefs of America, Japan, China and the Soviet Union. Meeting Henry Ford gave Father a chance to study modern industrial capitalism; 'with one lens they had a peep at the hundred percent efficiency of machine production' and 'through the other lens a glimpse of the suppression of the individuality of the workman, sensitive and even philosophical, who felt he was a diamond being used to cut glass'.

Later, on the same tour of 1934, Father went to see the Molotov works in the Soviet Union, where he found that 'the two main springs of human effort in the West, fear of unemployment and hope of financial reward had been removed'. His Russian guides told him that 'a belief in Bolshevism and all that it means for the uplifting of humanity had replaced both the carrot and the stick'. But in the book Father asked himself whether the alleged justification for what is called the dictatorship of the proletariat is not in fact the dictatorship of the Communist Party.

Neither Ford nor Stalin offered him a way he wanted to follow.

But a year later, in his election address in the 1935 campaign, when there were two million out of work, he told his constituents, 'There is no hope in this patching. A more rational approach must be made to our problems and it is to be found in the principle of socialism. Many [who] repudiate the word socialism yet approve the thing itself when they see it working . . . the forces of production need to be liberated and vitalised.' That was the authentic voice of the old 'gas-and-water socialism' (upon which he had been brought up as a municipal Progressive in East London) heard again in the middle of a world slump.

Smile! Smile! Smile!

To the Tune of "Pack up your Troubles."

Vote, vote for Wedgwood Benn
the LABOUR MAN,
And Smile, Smile, Smile,
He stands for Justice and the
People's Plan,
So smile boys, that's the style,
We want a Labour Government
To make our lives worth while,
So pile all your crosses on the
LABOUR MAN
And Smile, Smile, Smile,

BENN X

Father's leaflet for the 1935 General Election

Defeated in Dudley in the only campaign where he felt that corrupt methods were used against him, my father was finally elected in a by-election in Gorton in Manchester in early 1937. Back in the Commons, he threw himself into the campaign against appeasement and was elected top of Labour's Shadow Cabinet, which was a great tribute to the respect in which he was held by his colleagues.

When the war with Germany began, he felt that he ought to rejoin the services and in May 1940, at the age of sixty-three, when France fell, he applied to the RAF and was commissioned as a Pilot Officer, the lowest commissioned rank, and was posted to the Air Ministry, leaving my mother to carry on all his constituency work. Promoted later to Air Commodore, he went back to Italy (where he had served in the First World War), this time as a member of the Allied Control Commission. My dad was very fond of the Air Force and was extremely proud when his eldest son, my brother Michael, joined it and became a night-fighter pilot.

The following year Churchill asked Attlee to recommend three Labour MPs for inclusion in a special list of Labour peers. The announcement from Number 10 made the reasons clear: 'These creations are not made as political honours or awards but as a special measure of State policy. They are designed to strengthen the Labour Party in the Upper House.'

Father was very proud of the fact that his peerage was not an honour and, though it was a wrench to leave the Commons, he was back in uniform and he thought the Lords would be a useful place to continue in Parliament after the war. There were no life peerages at the time, and Father consulted my elder brother Michael (who would inherit the title) to find out whether he objected. He did not object because he planned to go into the

Church after the war. Father did not tell me about the peerage in advance, and I was angry about this.

Then in 1944 Michael died, and I became heir to the peerage. Father was overwhelmed by grief and determined to be active, so he flew home from Italy and got himself transferred to a new job, lecturing on the post-war world at RAF stations. He managed his itinerary so that it took him to Air Gunnery Schools, where he bullied the instructors to put him through a regular gunnery course, which he was able to do by virtue of his senior rank.

When he had completed his training, he arranged to visit airfields where bomber squadrons were stationed and flew on a number of air operations as a gunner in the rear turret, before he was discovered and grounded. He was sixty-seven and had earned a second mention in dispatches by the time he was demobilised in the summer of 1945, just before the General Election.

A few weeks later, after Labour came to power, Attlee made him Secretary of State for Air in his new Cabinet, and in his fourteen months there Father was particularly proud of one achievement. Having been sent to Egypt to lead the British delegation to renegotiate the 1936 Anglo-Egyptian Treaty, he felt his job was simply to end the British occupation of Egypt, which had soured Anglo-Egyptian relations for so long.

It was a cause he had believed in since he had served in Egypt in 1915, and though the final withdrawal from the Canal Zone did not take place until 1956, when he went to see President Nasser, he felt he had had some minor part in bringing it about.

Four years after I became an MP in 1950, Father took up the cause of a young constituent of mine called Paul Garland who was expelled from the Boy Scouts for being a communist. Father raised a debate in the Lords in which the Chief Scout, Lord

Rowallan, and almost every peer who spoke supported the expulsion of this young lad. Writing about it, he said:

> I will say quite simply what is my opinion. You can only conquer ideas with ideas . . . in the fresh air of freedom. This youth is sincere. We may think his opinions are in error but there is something more important than his opinions and that is his attitude. The conscience of a man, whatever his creed, is very precious, it is far stronger than acts of Parliament.

In 1958, two years before he died, he made a BBC broadcast and gave his own view of the role of Parliament. He interpreted his radicalism in these words: 'Parliament is more than an assembly. It is a workshop or, I should prefer to say, a battlefield. I have often tried to think why it is that when political issues arise I find myself instinctively holding opinions of a particular mould. I have had, so far, to be content with the explanation of the poet who declared "We do not choose our convictions, but they choose us and force us to fight for them to the death."'

Father was either tremendously buoyant or he would be 'on active service', as he called it, very serious and busy. But as he got older he was subject to depression and used to say, 'I'm not feeling very well today.' I would ask him, 'Would you like to go into the Lords and make a speech?' No. 'Would you like to go to Stansgate?' No. I too have periods of depression when I wonder if I have ever done anything worthwhile.

MOTHER

My mother was born in Scotland in 1897. Her religious convictions were the result of an interesting correlation of family experiences. Her Grandfather Holmes was a member of the Irvine Brethren, which meant a very severe start in life for her dad, who used to be dismissed with the phrase, 'Go to bed, Daniel, you've had enough pleasure for one day.'

This drove Daniel Holmes to atheism, but this atheism worried my mother. When she was a little girl of eight she said to herself, 'If there is no God, we were all born in an orphanage.' And so, on Sundays, she would go off on her own to the nearest Church of Scotland kirk, and from that developed her religious interest.

Mother had first visited the House of Commons in 1908, with her father and a Liberal MP; later, as a fourteen-year-old, she first saw my dad there. Afterwards she wrote to a London photographer and asked for photographs of some prominent MPs, including one of my father. However, it was not until after the war that she met him, when she was staying with her parents on the south coast and Father went to visit, using the excuse that he wanted to talk to his parliamentary colleague, but with his eyes on the young woman he wanted to marry.

When Mother married Father in 1920 he was a handsome man of forty-three, known as Captain Benn, decorated with the DSO and the DFC. He did not actually propose as such, but said, 'It would be quite easy – we could have a chop at the House every night', implying that he planned to marry her. She said, 'Yes, but what should I call you, Captain Benn?' She used his Christian name, Will – the name his wider family used – though his political friends called him Wedgie.

Mother was twenty years younger than Father, and she saw it as her duty to put Father's interests before hers. This she did until his death forty years later. She used to say that Father's existence was essential to her happiness, but his presence was not!

She became a teetotaller when she married, to comply with Father's wishes (not that she saw it as a sacrifice), but she insisted that alcohol was kept in the house for visitors. However, few ever came to the house for a meal, as my parents did not 'entertain' socially.

My father insisted that when they married, Mother should give up her favourite little dog, Dugald, a West Highland terrier. That, I think, was a hardship, for she was very fond of animals and used to see the dog occasionally afterwards, when it would whimper at her.

After they were married she visited his constituency of Leith, near Edinburgh, and went to a school with him. When the teacher said, 'And who has Captain Benn brought with him today?', the children called out, 'His daughter!'

On their honeymoon in Mesopotamia my father looked across a river (either the Euphrates or the Tigris, I am not sure which) and said, 'This reminds me of Stansgate!' – which was the place on the River Blackwater in Essex where his father had built a house, then sold it in 1903. Father always remembered how happy he had been there, and Mother discovered that he loathed holidays other than at Stansgate – a trait I picked up from him – so she took him to Maldon in Essex to stay at the Blue Boar. They went to Stansgate and met Captain Gray, an old sea captain, who then owned the house, and persuaded him to let them rent another house nearby for holidays. After Captain Gray's death, Father bought the house back in 1933, his attachment to Stansgate explaining why he took that name when he was made a peer.

Mother was a passionate believer in the rights of women, arguing against her own father who, even when women got the vote in 1918, said to her, 'We may have to take it away again, yet.' Although she called herself a suffragist rather than a suffragette, her theological interest and her campaigns for the rights of women led her to work as a young woman for the ordination of women in the Church of England, to which she had transferred when she married Father. The earliest movement devoted to this was called the League of the Church Militant and, while still a young woman, she met Dr Randall Davidson, Archbishop of Canterbury, at a dinner (he had been appointed Archbishop of Canterbury in Queen Victoria's reign) and was told by him to desist from such an idea, which only strengthened her own determination.

Later, as a delegate on behalf of the Church of England, at the ecumenical Amsterdam conference in 1948, Mother discovered that the conference was told she was not to be taken as representative of the Church on this matter, so she left the Church and joined the Congregationalists. Father was also passionate about equal rights for women. When he was appointed Secretary of State for Air in 1945, in order to support Mother's campaign, he appointed the first woman Chaplain in the Royal Air Force – Elsie Chamberlain, a Congregationalist minister. This greatly upset the then Archbishop of Canterbury, Geoffrey Fisher, who wrote to my father that he hoped that under no circumstances would a male Chaplain be required to take orders from a woman. Father discovered that when the Air Force list was published, the Revd Elsie Chamberlain had been put under the heading of 'Welfare Officer' instead of Chaplain, so he had the whole list pulped and reissued, with her in the proper place.

When the Congregationalists joined the Presbyterians to form the United Reformed Church, which appointed its ministers instead of electing them, as was the Congregationalist tradition, Mother joined with Elsie Chamberlain and others to form the Congregational Federation, of which she (Mother) became the first President.

I am very proud indeed to be the son of the first woman to be the head of a Christian denomination. Her influence in our family was immense: she was highly committed to the ecumenical movement and to inter-faith dialogue. In particular, she sought to eliminate from Christianity the traditional hostility to the Jews. She became a Fellow of the Hebrew University in Jerusalem, where a library is named after her.

Elsie gave the address at my father's funeral. Later, when Elsie died, I was honoured to be asked to give the address at her funeral and referred to these events, as well as to her distinguished service as Head of Religious Broadcasting at the BBC.

With all Mother's preoccupations outside the home, she developed no domestic skills at all. She and Father had a nurse for the children, a cook and servants to keep house, but Mother was not very good at handling domestic staff. When our first nurse, Nurse Parker, came to work for her, she became very depressed because the nurse would take us for a walk in our pram and speak of 'her children', which got Mother down. Eventually Nurse Parker had to go.

I never saw my mother cry; she was very 'Scottish', imbued with a strong Protestant ethic, and was not an openly emotional woman, although my father was sentimental and was easily moved to tears, as I am. When he was dying, he talked of his father a lot – 'My dad worked so hard, all those lectures he gave . . .' – and held my finger like a pencil and tried to write with it.

3

Life at Home

The Benn household when I was a child was, I suppose, fairly typical for a Cabinet minister and MP at the time. In comparison with most people (even middle-class people), we were well-off. Father's income in the 1920s was made up of his parliamentary salary plus a 'pension' of £500 per year from Benn Brothers, which he was given when he was first elected to Parliament in 1906, before MPs' salaries were introduced. He also had dividends from shares in Benn Brothers, although I do not know the exact amount of these.

As will become clear, Father – like Ernest – was very careful with money. His mother-in-law bought a Morris Oxford car for him in 1928 for £180 and that was our only car until 1954, when he bought another Morris Oxford!

The house I was born in, 40 Grosvenor Road, was on the Embankment looking south over the River Thames. In those days there were tugs going up and down, hooting as they pulled the barges full of goods that were being handled by the Port of London, which was then very active; that was long before the area became full of offices and fashionable flats. I used to imagine as a child that the barges were hooting at me for permission to pass.

Next door had lived Beatrice and Sidney Webb, and although I never remember meeting them, their role in the history of the Labour Party is a formidable one, since Sidney had drafted the famous Clause Four of the Labour Party's 1918 constitution, which committed us to 'the common ownership of the means of production, distribution and exchange'. It is a strange irony of history that when the houses in Grosvenor Road (which was by then renamed Millbank) were torn down in 1959, the Millbank Tower was built on that exact site, and became the headquarters of New Labour in the 1990s; and so it was there that Tony Blair succeeded in getting Clause Four removed from our constitution.

In 1928, when I was three, there was a huge flood in London and I remember looking out of the window and seeing boats sailing down the street in front of our house, which became completely flooded in the basement. Several people were killed in the flood, though fortunately no one from our house. We had to move out for a time to Greenock in Scotland, to Clydebank House, where my father was the Labour candidate for West Renfrewshire. When the mess in the basement was being cleared up, we discovered that a suitcase full of Sidney Webb's underwear had floated in from next door. I suppose that entitles me to claim that my political roots were based in Fabianism.

We returned to London in 1929 and for the next twenty years, until I got married and moved to Hammersmith, 40 Millbank (as it was renamed) was my home, apart from the war years and holidays at Stansgate in Essex.

It was a tall, five-storeyed house a few yards from the Tate

Gallery, next to a military hospital, and I used to see wounded soldiers from the First World War in their strange blue outfits with bright-red ties, still limping around and helping each other; one had been blinded, another would be pushing a wheelchair for a wounded comrade who had lost a leg. When we are told to support our boys in battle, we sometimes forget to look after them when they come home disabled.

We had a cook called, appropriately, Mrs Candy, who lived in the house with her husband and daughter Margaret, who was about the same age as my brother Michael. The Candys slept at the back of the house, next to my father's basement office. The kitchen acted as their living room.

On the top two floors were the rooms that made up the children's nursery. I remember that it was cold and the food was undistinguished. In August 1927 a piece appeared in *Nursery World* (owned by Benn Brothers) called 'Other People's Nurseries', describing:

. . . distempered walls of apple green, painted wooden huntsmen and hounds in full cry [which] tear around the picture rail. Mrs Benn drew my attention to the open grates for she thinks coal fires far better for children than more modern ways of heating . . . Michael who is five and three quarters is going to school when he is six; so he and Nanny are practising lessons. He showed me the sums he had been doing that morning, all perfectly neat and all quite right . . . Anthony ran fluently through one nursery rhyme after another. He has a wonderful memory and could talk when he was fourteen months old. We had more nursery rhymes, on the gramophone this time, till a march reminded the boys that they were going to be soldiers when they grew up. It was hard to believe that their rosy cheeks and brown limbs were gifts of a London sun but Nurse said that they almost lived in the Parks . . .

The reality was not quite so harmonious. Nurse Parker bullied my mother and was vaguely threatening if her demands were not met. She favoured me, and my elder brother definitely suffered as a consequence. Caroline concluded that many of my faults were the result of Nurse Parker's care, because afterwards I expected special treatment from everyone. I certainly recall weeping when she left, though I have only vague memories of her.

Our next nurse was Olive Winch, who was engaged by Mother in 1928. She was born on 1 January 1900, and she told us that her mother couldn't think of a name for her, so she picked on Olive because she had rubbed the new baby with olive oil. Nurse Olive had previously worked for the Horniman family and had also been in America working for a Mr Stuart, a journalist with the *New York Times*; she told us that on one occasion he had come back ashen-faced having witnessed an execution.

She lived at the top of our house, and was assisted by a series of nursery maids who also lived there. It seems odd now, but was common then for middle-class children to be left in the care of nannies for long periods at a young age. Earlier, I mentioned that in 1926 my parents had gone to visit the Middle East and Russia while I was a baby, and subsequently between 1931 and 1934 they were away on a tour of Germany, the USA, Japan, China and the USSR again.

Nurse Olive became a very close and intimate friend for well over sixty years, getting to know and love my own children. She was the daughter of a successful builder in Harlow, had been to the Norland Institute to be trained as a children's nurse, and under no circumstances was she to be referred to as a nanny! Apart from one month a year when she was on holiday, she was really in charge of our lives. As I have said Mother was busy as a theology student and campaigner for women's rights in the Church, and had no domestic skills beyond making tea and toast. When she had to cope on her own, her meals for us would comprise orange juice, cereal, tea and toast, which no doubt explains why that remains my favourite meal.

When my brother David became ill with what was thought to be TB of the intestines in 1935, Nurse Olive devoted herself completely to his care and recovery, moving with him to Bexhill and Bournemouth, and only leaving him during the war when she went to serve in a children's orphanage in London – where she was immensely popular.

We called her 'Nursey' and loved her dearly; my children used to stay with her in her retirement in Harlow, renaming her 'Buddy' – as it is the privilege of the young to do to the old. The Buddy stories she told them became part of family mythology. The one they most enjoyed was the story of the Three Pears: she had 'misheard' the Three Bears and created this ludicrous and unbelievable story about a big pear, a middle pear and a baby pear.

I continued this tradition, squeezing as much pathos as I could from stories to my children: the most shameless was the Daddy Shop story, about some children whose daddy was so busy that he couldn't play football with them or go on holiday, so one day they decided that they wanted a perfect daddy and took him back to the shop and asked for a new one. Their old daddy shuffled to the back of the shop and a brilliant new daddy appeared, with endless time to take them swimming, to the theatre and on holiday. But they began to miss their real daddy, so they went back to the Daddy Shop and asked for him back. The shopkeeper said, 'I don't know whether he is still there, I'll look.' He came back and there was real Daddy looking bent and sad, and a bit scruffy, and the children were so excited that they gave him a big hug and took him home. This used to produce floods of tears from my children – and even brought a few to my eyes. Caroline forbade me from telling it!

Another story of mine was about Tubby, a little man who lived in a house below the plughole in the bath. When the children were about to get into the bath, he would come out of his house, sit on a bar of soap and row up and down the water with two toothbrushes for oars. He became very friendly with my children and had a little pill that he gave them, which made them so small that they could go down with him to visit his house. When Caroline got into the bath and couldn't see the children, she noticed that they were on the bar of soap being rowed about by Tubby. Tubby also went to school with them, causing endless trouble, and even went out one day and put butter on the street so that the buses skidded and couldn't get up the hill. He had two cousins – one who lived in France, called M. Tubbé, and an Italian called Signor Tubbia – and was able to travel through the water pipes to visit them.

It was at Buddy's house in Harlow that, aged eighteen, I spent the last night with my brother Michael, sleeping in the same bed; our rest was disturbed because I had severe cramp and my brother dreamed that I was attacking him and reacted most vigorously. The following day I went with him to the airfield at Hunsdon in Essex where he was stationed, and he took me to the railway station for my return to London. My very last memory of him is as he cycled away when the train set off. Six months later he was dead.

Buddy continued to live in Harlow in her little house and we visited her there when she was bed-bound and could hardly speak, cared for by one of her nieces, to whom she had been immensely kind when that niece's marriage had broken up in South Africa and she had returned to Britain alone and without friends. Buddy died in 1992 and I spoke at her funeral, meeting again many of her family whom I had got to know as a child.

It goes without saying that Nursey was a very influential person in our young lives. My brothers and I had breakfast with her in the nursery. We had one meal a day with my parents in the dining room, the food being brought from the basement kitchen by a hand-operated lift. We were waited on at table.

I detested the food. I never liked meat and I loathed most of all turnips, parsnips and rice pudding. Many a time I was told I could not leave the table until I finished my rice pudding, which by then was cold and had a thick disgusting skin on it. It turned me against rice pudding and, to some extent, food itself ever since.

Life revolved around tea – early tea, breakfast tea, mid-morning tea, lunch with tea, dinner with tea and late-night tea.

When we were little we were sent to bed early every night. We had a small Bakelite radio in the nursery on which occasionally I used to listen to programmes such as *Monday Night at 8*; my father had a great walnut veneered radio in what was called the Green Room, which actually belonged to the house next door, but which Father rented and entered through a connecting door in the party wall.

Mother would come up at night and tell us Bible stories and

hear our prayers, which included prayers for the Spanish republicans during the Civil War and, when Father was out of Parliament
between 1931 and 1937, for 'Father getting back into Parliament';
and for 'the wall at Stansgate to be repaired' (being next to the
Blackwater estuary, the land was prone to flooding). When Mother
tucked us up in bed she would say 'Goodnight Darling, another
happy day tomorrow' even if we had had a flaming row that afternoon; the assumption that every day would be happy provided a
framework of security which was very reassuring.

I never remember being taken to a concert or the theatre, except
once to see *Peter Pan*. Although we lived next to the Tate Gallery,
I cannot even recall having been inside. My brother Dave told
me that when Father passed the Tate and considered going in,
what clinched his decision not to was that it would cost him
sixpence!

We were not allowed to have pets at home as children, but I
had three toy animals of which I was extremely fond: Big Teddy,
Little Teddy and Doggie. Doggie still lives in a cupboard at
Stansgate.

It was a happy childhood, but it changed when Dave fell ill
and went away to recuperate with Nurse Olive, leaving my brother
and me very lonely. Dave's illness was treated by our family doctor,
Alexander Bromley.

Our original doctor was a Dr Attlee, a relation of Clem's. I
don't remember him.

Dr Bromley was a Russian refugee who had come to England
with his brother and had then qualified medically. He became a
close friend of the family and it was he who gave David the idea
of learning Russian, in which David became fluent. He looked
after me when I had appendicitis, and I thought I had been put

to sleep by an 'atheist'. I subsequently learned that the anaesthetist in question was also an atheist – a story that amused Dr Bromley very much.

My mother thought that Jewish doctors were the best because they were interested in the patient rather than the disease, and I myself came to appreciate that when Caroline and I met our first NHS doctor, Dr Stein.

My mother's parents used to come and stay with us in Grosvenor Road because they had no fixed home and travelled continually, living mainly in hotels. When my mother was ill in bed once, and Michael and I were fighting, our grandmother said, 'If you don't stop fighting, your mother will die', which frightened us and greatly angered Mother.

Father's office was the centre of the house and everything revolved around it. It was not one room, but was spread over the first floor, ground floor and basement, with trapdoors and ladders built by him connecting the rooms, so that he could easily move up and down and consult and file his papers. His secretary Miss Triggs worked on the ground floor.

Father was a very serious student of national and international politics and developed the most elaborate filing system based on his daily and meticulous study of *The Times*. Three copies were delivered each day – two of the royal edition, so called because it was printed on rag paper that did not yellow with age. One copy was for my mother and the other two for my father: he would read them carefully, mark them with a decimal system of his own invention and then, by the use of huge guillotines, the newspaper pages were cut, moved over little rollers with sticky paste and stuck onto pages that were then inserted into loose-leaf files appropriate to the subject.

His indexing system, rather like the Dewey system, was based on giving a number to each subject, all of which were cross-referenced for ease of consultation. For example, his personal files were 101, and Russia, as far as I remember, was 10065. He devised this system because he used to refer, somewhat contemptuously, to a normal filing system where Alcoholism would be filed under A, Drunkenness under D and Teetotalism under T, with various miscellaneous and urgent files under M and U! Such a system – which he sometimes, possibly unfairly, attributed to his brother Ernest – made it impossible Father thought to find anything quickly.

All my personal files from the time when I was a child until now have always also been marked 101, and some of my children have used 101 for their personal files, too.

The task of reading, marking, cutting, gluing and filing the day's news according to their subject took a great deal of his time and Miss Triggs's, but it meant that at any moment he could pull out any file and remind himself of what *The Times* had said on the subject over the previous twenty years, with some contempt for those colleagues in Parliament who allowed the day's banner head-lines to shape their thinking.

The guillotines and gluing machines, though invented by my father and very amateurish, made his basement office into a mini-factory; but they did not have the necessary safety precautions that would now be required by law. On one occasion, one of the really big guillotines – whose size can be gauged by the fact that it was able to cut a page of *The Times* from top to bottom in one deadly swoop – fell on my older brother Michael and cut a slice off the side of his thumb. He put it in a bottle of alcohol and showed it proudly to reluctant family members and visitors, who found the whole thing disgusting and felt that my father had been highly irresponsible.

This passion for keeping things reached absurd limits, as when I had my appendix out, aged thirteen, and put it in a little bottle of formaldehyde and brought it to the table. This led my father to make a set of appendixes for all members of the family, so that one day when I came to lunch there were little bits of vegetable in bottles of cold tea, one for each member of the family.

We only had one telephone in the house – VICtoria 0078 – the number presumably indicating the low coverage of the telephone at the time it was installed. Because Father wanted to be able to phone and work at the same time, he acquired from the Post Office a telephone operator's headset, which was very big and cumbersome and drove my mother mad because when she answered the phone the headset messed up her hair, which had to be brushed back into position.

Father's great passion was for what he called 'improvements' and the house was full of them, normally installed by a jobbing carpenter who did his best to make possible the extraordinary ideas my father had as to how a house should be constructed.

For example, just outside one of his offices he built a cupboard in the ceiling and all his clothes were hung on coathangers attached to a bar, which with the aid of a pulley could be hauled up and out of sight. The rope had to be released to allow him to choose what suit he was going to wear that day.

As a twelve-year-old, I remember getting into serious trouble when we had a visit from his parliamentary colleagues and, in order to interest them, I opened the cupboard door and released his clothes, so that they all came down. Although this aroused a great deal of amusement, as you can imagine, it did not go down very well with my mother.

Most of the visitors to the house were connected with Father's work. For instance, on one occasion the Maharaja of Alwar, whom Father had met while Secretary of State for India, came. He was charming and told us stories about hunting tigers, and he gave me an Indian prince's outfit with a turban, a jewelled jacket and white breeches, the remains of which are still rotting in a box at Stansgate. I later discovered that he had been a brute in his own state, and I think he was subsequently murdered in France. Another visitor was Reinhold Niebuhr, the American theologian, who had married Ursula, an English student. They were firm family friends.

We were governed by Victorian principles of prudence and economy. Father always turned the lights out and we were rebuked for leaving them on. The greatest offence that we could commit was to WASTE TIME!

Despite this rather grim account, he was the most amusing man I have ever met, with a great sense of humour, a capacity to tell stories and play practical jokes that would have done credit to a teenager, and listening to him was always enormous fun.

STANSGATE

All of our holidays have been at Stansgate, on the Blackwater estuary in Essex, since I was a child. My father loved the house and the location; Stansgate also became his title in the Lords, which has given the impression that it is an ancient stately home, and that I came from one of the oldest aristocratic families in Britain – a myth nurtured by the tabloids for their own political purposes.

My father spent his childhood summers there sailing on the river and taking part in plays, which his father wrote and which were enacted in the garden.

We had no mains water supply when I was a child and we depended on a windmill to raise water from our well, using oil lamps to light the house and wood fires to heat it.

There was a disused slaughter house, which my father had bought from a nearby farmer, and it was there that he moved his archives from London when the house in Millbank caught fire in 1940. It would be more interesting to claim that we had been victims of the Blitz, but the real reason for the fire was that, in order to save money, my father had asked my brother Michael (who was then in his late teens) to rewire his office and it had not been done safely. Happily, most of the papers were safe, and during the war my brother and I moved them to this old slaughter house, and Father spent many happy hours going over them. At Stansgate we swam and cycled and did a bit of sailing, and Father used to sit with us and reminisce about the old days.

My brothers and I did not have any pets in London, but there was a little puss called Fluffy living locally at Stansgate, which my brother and I smuggled into the car to take back to London. On the way back my father discovered this kitten and was furious – he stopped the car, knocked at a cottage and asked the woman who lived there to take it. We were very upset. Father had strong ideas about what was, and what was not, in order.

On another occasion at Stansgate my brother David gave a local boy my set of toy soldiers while I was away. I loved those soldiers – I would dig trenches and sew sandbags, and would advance and withdraw the soldiers in my own little stories. When David gave them away I was so angry that I rushed at him and bit him; he screamed and I was punished, and the other boy had to return the soldiers.

The house at Stansgate was a pre-fabricated wooden structure built by Boulton and Paul, at a cost of £600, which had been floated downriver for construction and originally had a thatched roof. Captain Gray had this replaced by tiles, and covered the outside with expanded metal and then pebble-dashed it to give it greater strength.

There were various outbuildings, including the windmill, a garage and a circular wooden summer house which we used to call 'The Temple', where Mother would work when she wanted to escape from the family. The farm was next door and we used to milk the cows and go out on the tractor at harvest time, and ask for a ride on the horses that drew the waggons as the hay was collected and built up into hayricks for winter feed.

Father had acquired an old ship's lifeboat, which he named the *Brethren*, and we used to sail in the Blackwater. It had strong tides and muddy beaches on which, if we got stuck, we had to wait for the tide to come in and float us off many hours later, for the mud was like quicksand and could trap you, making escape impossible.

We sailed to Osea Island, just opposite; down to Bradwell, where the long lines of deserted merchant ships lay at anchor because of the Depression; or up to Maldon, from where the fishing smacks came out each day, returning later with their catches.

Osea Island itself was fascinating, with a pier along which were gun emplacements to defend the river in the First World War; facing us across the river was the big house built by Charrington, who gave up his fortune as a brewer, and turned the house into a home for recovering alcoholics.

There was a simple causeway connecting Osea to the mainland, used for the delivery of supplies, and when the tide was low the causeway would appear. The postman would cycle across with letters to deliver and collect from the postbox, which bore the unique inscription: 'Letters collected according to the tide.'

Here, as in London, Father was always making 'improvements' with the help of a local joiner. For example, all the rooms at Stansgate interconnected – so that you could enter the bathrooms from both ends, which was not always altogether comfortable!

The nearest village was Steeple, with the Star Inn and the Sun and Anchor, a little church and two chapels, one being established for a dissenting sect called the Peculiar People and the other Congregational. There my grandmother had paid for a notice board on which it was announced that marriages could be 'Solomonized' – an innocent misprint that conveyed the wrong impression of the sanctity of monogamous marriage.

Also in Steeple was Mr Harrington, the cobbler, who worked in a little thatched shed and would cut our hair for sixpence, which seemed a lot at the time.

Mrs Hipsey had a cottage where she took in washing, and in 1945 we collected from her the laundry we had left there to be washed in 1939 – and it had all been done and kept carefully.

Along the street was Mr Dash, who had a horse and cart and advertised his work with the simple words painted on the shed next door: 'DASH 1868', which remained there for many years.

Further away was Southminster and occasionally we would go to Maldon, or even Chelmsford, which seemed like a teeming metropolis compared to Steeple.

We sat on the lawn, played games, sunbathed, collected chalk and pebbles from the beach and swam in the river, which was at that time clean enough to do so safely.

Once a week we had a musical evening and I would play some 78 rpm records on an old gramophone – all of which are still in my possession – and we would sit and drink tea (or rather the grown-ups did, because I was not allowed to drink tea or coffee until I was twelve, on the same day that I wore long trousers for the first time).

Stansgate was – and still is – my idea of a real holiday and, apart from a one-day trip to Boulogne, I never went abroad until my war service; the happiest time for me is to have my children and grandchildren down for a weekend and discuss with them more and more improvements.

4

Growing Up

When I was born in 1925, my father was, as I said, the Liberal Member of Parliament for Leith. Two years later he left the Liberals, resigned his seat and joined the Labour Party. In 1928 he was asked to stand for Aberdeen and was successfully elected there in a by-election.

In that year, when I was three and a half, I visited the home of a Labour MP, Sir Oswald Mosley, who had joined Labour from the Conservatives. I must have been invited to a children's party, although I don't remember that; Mother recalled that we regularly played with Cynthia and Oswald Mosley's children, so presumably that was why we were there. I remember there were enamelled fire 'dogs' – one in the shape of a soldier and one a sailor – and at the end I was asked to say thank you and said, 'Boys and girls and sailors, thank you for a nice tea': my first speech. Mother had no time for 'Tom' Mosley, as he was known, or the British Union of Fascists, which he later formed.

In June 1930, at the age of five (by which time my father was in the Cabinet as Secretary of State for India), I went to 10 Downing Street to watch the Trooping of the Colour from the balcony, and Ramsay MacDonald gave me a chocolate biscuit. My mother told me that I said afterwards, 'I expected to meet the Prime Minister, but I didn't expect a chocolate biscuit.'

Ramsay MacDonald had been left a widower with five young children, and by the time he was Prime Minister for the second time, his daughter Ishbel acted for him as his host at Number 10. In her hand-written letter of invitation to my mother to take us to see the Trooping of the Colour, she added:

> Of course if it is against your principles to make them picture soldiers as fine fellows belonging to a good institution I shall quite understand. I should like to have an anti military lecture for the children after the show, but I think I had better leave that to the parents.

Father had devoted his period at the India Office to an attempt to bring about Indian self-government, for which he was sharply criticised by Churchill. It was at Father's initiative that a Round Table conference was arranged in London in late 1931 to discuss the future of India. In the election in October that year, Labour was heavily defeated and my father lost his seat. Nevertheless he took me to meet Mahatma Gandhi with my older brother Michael, and I remember the occasion vividly because Gandhi, who was sitting on the floor on a carpet, invited us to sit down next to him. Though I don't remember what he said, I was much struck by the power of the man who both defeated the British empire and reconciled the British to their defeat – as Archbishop Desmond Tutu later attempted with his policy of Truth and Reconciliation.

When Father lost his North Aberdeen seat, he sent Michael a very sweet telegram from Scotland, saying:

+ + MUCH MORE TIME FOR GAMES NOW = DADDY + +

The 1935 election was the first which I remember and in which I was involved. I thought of myself as a socialist at an early age, although I did not really understand what 'socialism' meant. I distributed a little book called *Fifty Reasons Why You Should Vote Labour*. It cost one penny and on each page was a different policy, such as:

No. 1 The Peace Act: Once it was passed no Government without violating the law of the land could resort to war as an instrument of national policy.

No. 15 National Transport: The duty of the National Transport Board would be to bring all forms of transport together to give the public good service and the employees a fair deal.

No. 26 Land Ownership: A primary step towards the national planning of agriculture is to bring all agricultural land under public ownership.

No. 41 Child Welfare: Labour's Policy is to provide more and better infant welfare centres and to develop, on a large scale, open-air nursery schools.

FIFTY REASONS WHY YOU SHOULD VOTE LABOUR

Prices:
1 copy, 1½d. post free
12 copies, 10d. "
100 " 6s. 8d. "

from

THE LABOUR PUBLICATIONS DEPT.
Transport House,
Smith Square, London, S.W.1

October 1935

3.—DISARMAMENT

Labour stands for drastic disarmament by rapid stages through international agreement.

A Labour Government would maintain such defence forces as are necessary and consistent with our membership of the League.

But the best defence is not huge competitive armaments, but the organisation of collective security and the agreed reduction of national armaments everywhere.

> Labour has not "abandoned hope." It would make a fresh effort, and, in particular, would propose to other nations the complete abolition of all national air forces, the effective international control of civil aviation and the creation of an international air force.

I also distributed a leaflet issued by the Mineworkers Federation (fore-runner of the NUM) describing the deaths and injuries in the pits in the nine years following the general strike when the coal owners were dominant and were supported by the National Government. Having kept it in my archives I had it copied and reissued it, fifty years later during the miners' strike in 1984–5, as a warning of what was at stake.

THE PRICE OF COAL

7,839 KILLED
1,200,042 INJURED

That is the price of Coal for the years 1927-34. The dead include 231 boys under 16, 320 lads between 16 and 18, and 294 lads between 18 and 20. The killed and injured include 199,612 lads and boys under 20.

GREATER OUTPUT	LOWER WAGES
The output of coal per man per shift has increased by nearly a third since 1924, but wages per	man have gone down by nearly a sixth. Thousands receive less than 40/- per week.

THE MINERS' CLAIM

THE MINERS CLAIM AN EXTRA 2/- PER SHIFT,
THEY OFFER TO ABIDE BY THE DECISION OF
INDEPENDENT ARBITRATORS.

——THE COALOWNERS HAVE REFUSED INDEPENDENT
ARBITRATION.

——THE "NATIONAL" GOVERNMENT HAS ALSO REFUSED
TO TAKE ACTION.

——THE "NATIONAL" GOVERNMENT IS ALWAYS ON
THE SIDE OF THE COALOWNERS.

THE MINERS DEMAND A LIVING WAGE

My first visit to the House of Commons was on 22 February 1937 to see Father take his seat for Gorton, which he had won in a by-election that month. He introduced me to Lloyd George, and to Clement Attlee, who had become the new Labour leader.

Going back to 1932, after the General Election my parents decided to visit Marburg in Germany for two months, where Father wished to learn German and Mother continued to study Hebrew. My mother described how suspicious the German authorities were of her interest in Judaism. It was on the eve of Hitler coming to power, and my parents came back with vivid accounts of the conduct of the Hitler Youth and the danger that was posed to democracy; they brought back with them a vinyl record of the Nazi anthem, the 'Horst Wessel' song, which I think I still have somewhere.

I remember listening to one of Hitler's ranting speeches from Nuremberg being broadcast on the radio, and by the end of the 1930s it was clear that war was inevitable – an idea that had already formed in my mind when I read *Mein Kampf*, a book I still have on my shelves next to the autobiography of Mussolini (whose ideas are now back in fashion with the neo-conservatives who have reappeared in the West). I also have in my possession a booklet issued by the Home Office in 1938 entitled 'The Protection of your house against air-raids', which advised: '. . . if the head of the house will consider himself as "captain of the ship" and put these air raid precautions into effect the principal object of this book will have been achieved'. From that it was clear that war was considered a serious possibility. When, aged fourteen and a half, I sat at Stansgate and listened to Neville Chamberlain's announcement that we were at war with Germany, it was with a great deal of foreboding, but a sense of the inevitable.

By 1939 I was at Westminster School, but my first school (in 1931) was a mixed infants called Graham Street School, which was attached to the Frances Holland School for Girls. My main recollection of it is looking with admiration at the big girls, aged seven to eleven, who dominated the place and made us infants feel rather inadequate. I cannot recall many of the teachers, but the head teacher was Miss Morison, who ran the school very efficiently and always took an interest in me, which I appreciated. The fees were thirteen guineas a term; milk and biscuits were three shillings, dancing two and a half guineas, and extra Latin and arithmetic coaching were five shillings an hour.

The other teacher who made an impact on me was Miss Babcock, who taught religious education, and with whom I had a clash at the first class (when I was five). Miss Babcock said in

Bible Studies that 'God was angry', and I jumped up and said, 'God is love'. As a result of this, I was sent to an empty classroom during all her lessons to read some child's book about the Bible. Miss Babcock explained to my mother, 'The trouble with Anthony is that when I begin, he begins!' I still remember the misery of sitting in that room on my own.

I sympathise with Miss Babcock now, but at the time she was a fearsome woman with a bun, who frightened me. Unfortunately, she did not deal with the main problem – that I was too talkative.

The only prize I ever won at school was the Toplady Prize for Divinity at Westminster and I still have the book – a Bible – with the inscription inside it. I wasn't very clever at school and my parents did not take much interest in my progress.

My school reports from the Graham Street School started off quite well: 'Writing: Good and careful'; 'French: Très bien'; 'History: Very good'; 'Conduct: Very good'. But by 1932 a note of disapproval had crept in: 'Writing: This needs great care'; 'Conduct: Generally very good but is apt to be too noisy and excited.' At the end of 1932 my conduct was 'Generally very good but is still lacking self-control'. By the time I left in the summer of 1933, all subjects were reasonably good.

An event I remember clearly at infant school was a nativity play, in which I was allocated a very small role as a shepherd whose job it was to stand quietly at the back. But I told my parents I had a much larger role, and they came to watch the play, though they did not even see me. I got into trouble for pinching the bottom of a shepherdess next to me, whose name I now forget.

I was taken to, and brought home from, school each day by car, driven by Father's secretary Miss Triggs, who represented

Authority. On one occasion she forgot to collect me, and I recall having lunch with the big girls and crying when Miss Triggs turned up to collect me with a peremptory apology.

It was an Anglican school and we used to go out for walks nearby in the Royal Hospital in Chelsea and look at the Chelsea Pensioners in their red coats and tricorne hats; they looked so very old with a mass of medals on their chests, which they would have earned during the First World War and maybe even the Boer War. Every year the Chelsea Flower Show was held there (as now), and we used to see the preparations, although I never actually went to the Flower Show myself.

From there I was moved to a preparatory school known as Gladstone's, in Cliveden Place, on the other side of Sloane Square, at which we had to wear green blazers and green caps and were marched out for our daily exercise. Mr Gladstone, whom we were told was a relative of the Grand Old Man, looked the part.

Our rival school was Gibbs, whose pupils wore red blazers and caps, and although I do not recall any competitive sporting activity, we saw them as rivals and occasionally passed these red-coated children and congratulated ourselves on being at Gladstone's. There was also the McPherson gymnasium near the school, where I took part in boxing matches. I fought one boy, Neville Sandelson, who later became a Labour MP and then joined the SDP.

Gladstone's used to go every week to the Liverpool Victoria Sports Ground at Acton, where we played cricket and football, and it was there that I first saw a helicopter – I think it was actually an autogyro with a circulating blade at the top. On one occasion there was a fathers' cricket match, which my dad attended, and, in a very mischievous way, when he was sent in to bat, he asked my teacher Mr Leman which end of the bat he should hold. This caused me great embarrassment, much amusement among the teachers and amazement among my fellow pupils.

Sexual education was virtually non-existent and we formed a Sex Society to discuss these matters. When I asked Mother questions she would reply, 'Darling, it is so beautiful I can't tell you about it.' If I asked Father, he would say, 'Ask your mother!'

When Mr Gladstone's time was coming to an end, the school was renamed Eaton House and moved a few yards along from Sloane Square. One day we were told that the American Ambassador, a Mr Kennedy, had in mind sending his son to the school. This child must have been JFK's younger brother, although in the event he did not come to the school.

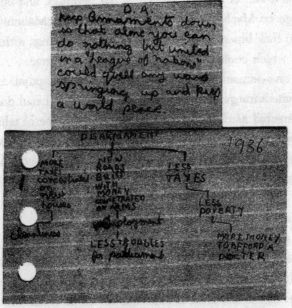

An early political paper: my thoughts on disarmament in 1936

I was allowed to go to Gladstone's by bus, and a route was planned that permitted me to get there without crossing the road, although it did involve a diversion from the direct route. I was given my fare every morning to pay for the ticket. In those days the buses were owned by different companies – for instance, the red open-decked buses of the General Omnibus Co., and the chocolate-coloured double-deckers owned by Thomas Tilling. I realised that if I took a different route from the one I had been told to take, I could save about tuppence a day and so, without telling my parents, I saved the money and spent it at Woolworths. This was discovered when a bus ticket in my coat revealed that I was not catching the authorised bus route – I had a lot of explaining to do.

I was leader of a group known as the Bennites, and our rivals were led by MacMahon, who organised the MacMahonites. We used to flick bits of paper at each other, using slings with rubber bands, which could sting very sharply at short range.

On one occasion I stole a pencil from a fellow pupil. I was so overcome with guilt that I told my father what I had done and he contacted Mr Leman about it. The importance of telling the truth was instilled in me as an essential requirement, then and throughout life. I subsequently wrote to my father, who must have been away from home in 1935:

Dear Daddy

I got your letter and I am really sorry about the untruth. I have honestly decided to turn over a new leaf . . . Mr Leman was very kind to me and what he told me impressed me, it was decent of you to get him to talk to me as I realise it was for the good.

At Gladstone's, I did not particularly excel: 'English: Too slap-dash'; 'Drawing: No artist but he is keen'; 'Arithmetic: Rather inaccurate and should be neater'. By the time I was twelve, at the end of 1937, Mr Leman wrote of my general conduct:

> Anthony is a little too conscious of 'Anthony'. He works well and tries hard, but has a tendency to overdo things . . . Next term I shall watch him with interest – he *ought* to be good.

From there I went on to Westminster School as a day-boy and, incredible as it is to report, I had to go to school every day in a top hat and tailcoat; I was there from 1938 to 1942. Westminster was equally conservative and we even had the son of the German Ambassador, von Ribbentrop, at the school. My brother Michael was already at Westminster when I moved there, and the day-boys were very fortunate in not having to board in dormitories. I think public-school boys have always found prison easy because the accommodation and discipline are familiar.

Westminster was a very old foundation and I had the experi-ence of prayers in Westminster Abbey every day. I learned the Lord's Prayer and others in Latin, and they had a comfortable ritual feel. The organ was played by Mr Lofthouse, and the Abbey became a very familiar place to me, although I do not recall going there for services. I do remember watching the coronation of George VI in 1937 from outside the House of Commons.

My housemaster was Mr C. H. Fisher, a very jovial man, who had the responsibility of teaching me about sex. There were no girls at Westminster School, so they continued to be a mystery, although Mr Fisher had taken me aside at the end of one day to give me a clinical explanation. By then I had seen a few bulls, cows and dogs in action, had exchanged smutty stories with my schoolmates and had a fairly clear idea, even though this was never explicitly linked to the species to which I belonged. It was in marked contrast to my own grandchildren's understanding, because they seem to know every detail from the age of about seven. Mr Fisher was known as Preedy because he smoked Preedy's tobacco in his pipe; later he married the matron.

Another teacher was Mr Carlton, who later became headmaster, and was known as Coot. On one occasion my father asked Coot to come out with us to the cinema and took us afterwards to a milk bar, which I thought was a night club. Father no doubt chose the milk bar because it was cheap.

Another of our teachers was Mr Wordsworth, known as Siggy, a descendant of the poet. We also had a science teacher called Mr Rudwick, who was known as Beaker, and we called his children 'Beaker's experiments'. I didn't like science; my main interest was politics, although we were never taught it as a subject.

The headmaster of Westminster, Mr J. T. Christie, later became the principal of Jesus College Oxford and was inevitably known as Jesus Christie. He was very tall and he gave us a moral education which he hoped would influence us for the rest of our lives.

One lecture he gave was on the importance of 'keeping our minds clean'. He said, 'There are three rooms in your mind: the front room, where your thoughts are known to all your friends. You must keep it clean and tidy. Your back room, where you have private thoughts which you do not need to disclose but also must be clean and pure. If in the basement you keep a lot of smelly vegetables that are rotten, the smell will come up and infect your back room and your front room and you must always remember that.' One boy, who was known to be homosexual and had a relationship with another pupil, commented on this speech by saying, 'But I keep my smelly vegetables in the front room!'

There was quite a lot of homosexuality, in the sense that some of the boys were actively gay and others were prepared to go along with it. There was gossip, but not much was made of it. I dare say the headmaster had this in mind when he lectured us.

The school had a rowing team – we rowed from one of the boathouses at Putney. I did of course support Oxford in the boat race because I intended to go there. I enjoyed fencing, and did épée fencing, but was never really enthusiastic about any sport.

I loved the Boy Scouts and my Scout Master, Godfrey Barber, was a pacifist, a good, kind man. We had a Scout camp in Oban, Scotland, and lived in tents. Mr Barber developed a 'wet latrine' where, instead of peeing into the ground, he got us to cut a little trench and fill it with pebbles. We stood by the trench and peed into it, protected from public view by a canvas screen just in front of the trench.

When a visiting Scout Commissioner came to see us he made use of this, but totally misunderstood the principle, and stood on the pebbles and peed against the canvas screen. He declared he had never seen such a good Scout latrine!

When I decided that, with the approach of war, I should transfer from the Scouts to the Air Training Corps, Mr Barber was very disappointed. We had an exchange of correspondence about this, in which he wrote:

With regard to the ATC I came to the view that if it must take place simultaneously with scout meetings, boys who feel bound to join would have to leave the troop . . . So I'm afraid we must lose you, and I expect you will start at the beginning of next term . . .

Yours ever

S. M.

PS Your journey report, by the way, omitted all bearings and distances.

I felt I should prepare myself for military service. During the war pacifism was a controversial idea, to the extent that the League of Nations Association – an organisation rather like the UN today – was regarded as suspect.

There was a student group at Westminster called UFPF (which stood for the United Front for Progressive Forces), known as the Uff Puffs, which was influenced by the growing anti-fascist movement with which Stafford Cripps was associated. I threw myself into the junior debating society and we discussed the case for and against appeasement; I took a critical view of the Munich settlement that Chamberlain had just negotiated with Hitler.

Westminster School was evacuated, first to Lancing College in Sussex and then, in the summer of 1940 when France fell, to Exeter University.

Although I had an expensive private education, which was normal for upper-middle-class children at the time and was intended to prepare me for a well-paid job of some kind, I find, on looking back, that it did not help me much in later life. What I learned in the Air Force, as a constituency MP and by observation gave me a far better opportunity of understanding the world in which we live than the schooling that I received.

I was never a great reader at school and cannot remember many books being read to me as a child. I had one book on my shelves called *Theras, The Story of an Athenian Boy*. I also remember a book that I think my uncle gave me, about two people on a desert island who ended up pricing everything: instead of exchanging potatoes for wood, or whatever, one of the men said, 'Let's work out the relative value . . .' A sort of textbook for capitalism. And I adored a picture-book called 'A Naval Alphabet' with wonderful colour plates.

H for the Hammock, the sailorman's bed.
They are not so hard as they look, it is said.

There is no room in the ships for beds for all the sailors, so they sleep in hammocks made of canvas, and which can be put out of the way in the daytime. At night they are hung on two hooks overhead. They are very comfortable when you get used to them.

My attitude towards women – 'females', as I called them then – was very backward, as the following reference in my journal for 1942, when I was seventeen, shows:

The theory of friendship with females

I cannot say that I really understand females yet, therefore I am not really qualified to write. What I have found out however I will put down.

Silence, quietness, modesty and honesty count very much. The sort of person required [by females] is one who is very friendly, leaves most of the talking to the other person, speaks not of himself, is scrupulously honest and upright, has a ready sense of humour and who is gentlemanly. That is to say helps them on with their coats, opens the door for them, gives up his seat for them, pays for them everywhere. This is very primitive . . . and makes females look so as well. Later I may understand them better.

Subsequently I wrote about the difference in my attitude towards boys and girls:

With girls I feel romantic. Of course there is no lasting element in it and I know it, but I seem to love them. Whenever I meet a respectable looking girl, I think I have fallen in love with her. I don't quite understand it. Contrary to my feeling to male friends, I have no desire to discuss politics or religion . . . It is a thing of emotions, not of interest or reason.

As a teenager, I wrote in my journals the most elaborate, stumbling analyses of 'how to approach females', comparing friendships with them to friendships with 'males' and trying to distinguish between physical attraction and relationships based on shared interests and understanding – passages that look absurd now, but which reflected someone brought up in a family of boys by Victorian parents, and who went to an all-boys school.

In 1942, at the height of the war, Mother and I went to stay at my Uncle Ernest's old home, Blunt House, by then a girls' school. I was sixteen or seventeen and there was a girl whom I liked very much; I tried to get into her bed, in the dormitory. Not surprisingly, the offence was discovered and raised with my mother, who must have been very embarrassed. Most unfairly, the girl involved was punished, whereas I was not. In a letter she wrote to me after the 'incident' she said:

> PS. Just a short note at the end. Miss X really blamed me for the whole thing, [unreadable] that you were so young and hadn't met many girls and that I should have been firm and refused but how could I have? In fact according to her I led you astray.

During the war I wrote to my brother, who was serving in North Africa, and said that I thought of subscribing to a girls' magazine called *Girl's Own Paper*, but discovered it was full of advice on dressmaking and cookery that wouldn't really have helped me.

I once asked my father, when I was about twelve, what buggery was, and with a look of extreme embarrassment he said, 'It is two men trying to have a baby.' Even at that age I knew this was nonsense and, when I told Father that, he referred me back to Mother, who I suspect had never heard of it.

At some stage I think a booklet was smuggled into my room called 'Straight Talks to a Boy on Growing Up', which I seem to recall consisted of very sketchy descriptions of the way that babies came to be born, accompanied by dire warnings against masturbation. It quoted the advice given to Boy Scouts, which was that if desire gets too strong, try plunging your arms up to the elbows in cold water – a remedy I never tried, but which I suspect would not have worked.

From 1937 and 1938 I have poems and letters that I never sent, with declarations of passion: 'to my love Pauline, I dream every night of you'; 'Hether [sic] Betty Harper whose laughing eyes and flowing black hair and sporting decency are in a class of their own'; 'Name-not-yet-known whose calm dignity and graceful movement made a true case of love at first sight'.

I did have embedded in my mind for many years, right into my late teens, that if you even kissed a girl delicately on her cheeks, you had to marry her – a thought that held me back on many occasions, for fear that marriage with children might prove a disaster. I sometimes wish my eight-year-old granddaughter had been available to advise me when I was eighteen.

A normal and open attitude towards sex seems to me to be so obvious, and when Caroline and I were asked about it by our own children, we answered frankly, but maybe in some trepidation, waiting for the next question. This was usually 'What are we having for dinner tonight, Dad?', which indicated that the basic information provided had satisfied their curiosity.

One long-term effect was to convert me to the importance of co-education, because if children are segregated at school, they are denied any understanding of the opposite sex and of the respect that is due between men and women throughout later life.

5

Michael, David and Jeremy

The all-boys culture of senior school was reinforced by my being born into a family of boys. Michael was born in 1921, I came along in 1925, David in 1928 and Jeremy in 1935.

Michael was a very thoughtful person and someone to whom I looked up with great respect, even though, like all brothers, we had fierce arguments that sometimes led to blows. Once he seized a copy of *Mein Kampf*, which I had bought when I was about twelve, and tore it apart so that, when I read it now, I have to struggle to keep the pages from flying out. He was a keen sportsman and used to row on the Thames with the Westminster Eight, which impressed me greatly.

Influenced by my mother, Michael became very religious and, when he was at school, established a prayer circle. He used to send duplicated messages, a copy of one of which I still have. A text written in purple ink on a piece of shiny paper was turned upside-down and pressed on a jelly-like substance; further copies could be made by pressing blank pieces of paper on the jelly, which then reproduced the writing in a very faint purple colour.

In 1940, when he was nineteen, Michael went up to Gorton, Manchester, where my father was then the Labour MP, but was away at the war; Mother was standing in for Father at meetings. From there he wrote to me, 'Mother is unfortunately ill and I am doing the work which she was to have done this week. Naturally I am a little apprehensive at addressing so many meetings, especially as the first one is in a church and I shall find myself in a pulpit.' He was very competent at such a young age. A few days later he wrote, 'I had quite an enjoyable time in Gorton. I spoke for about 50 minutes three times, though I was compelled to be a bit shorter on two evening meetings on account of air raids.'

In March 1941, following the small, private prayer circle that he had formed, and from many airfields where he was subsequently stationed, he found time to send advice to those who were carrying on that work. In one letter he set out his views on the role that Christian fellowship could play, and how it might be explained to others:

March 24th 1941: Here are a group of people who are trying to live Christian lives and grow up into Christian men and we find that by meeting together we derive more benefit and help than by remaining separate. If you think you could also derive benefit from joining us, then do come.

We ask no standard of people but we realise we are all probably at different stages of advancement.

You are entirely free to leave and come back just as you wish. We shall force no ideas down your throat and the only thing we shall demand from you is genuine and liberal tolerance towards people with whose ideas you do not agree.

That is most important. It was the thing we learned first . . . For we believe that in religious matters it is essential for the individual to exercise full and unprejudiced choice.

Long before his death, Michael had resolved that, if he survived the war, he would seek ordination and become a Christian minister, and his letters dealt at length with both religion and politics.

Of course, many of his letters to me were about service life and his hopes that he would be able to qualify as a pilot, which he did, serving first as a night-fighter pilot flying Beaufighters and later on Mosquitoes.

On one occasion, when his aircraft developed a fault, he had to bale out over the Scottish moors. He wrote about this from RAF Accrington on 28 March 1942, 'It was a nice moonlight night and we flew around for about half an hour while making up our minds on the best course to take. Eventually, we agreed that we should jump.' Arthur (Michael's navigator) came forward, opened the front door, said goodbye and jumped:

I called up goodbye on the wireless and went too. It was very thrilling though over very quickly.

I stood at the hatch and disconnected myself from everything and then allowed the slip stream to blow me away. I had my hand on the rip cord and I somersaulted twice before I pulled it. It opened with a bit of a jerk and before I fully realised what had happened, I was dangling in the moonlight over the moors of Scotland.

I had landed very heavily on soft moss and after a moment to regain my breath was none the worse.

Michael said it was two hours before he found a house, where a woman took him in and gave him food: 'It took a good deal to finally allay their suspicions that I was not a German but fortunately I was not shot at or piked to death.'

After his tours of duty in Britain, Michael was sent to North Africa, where he shot down four German planes and was decorated with the DFC, took part in the landings in Salerno, and for a period was attached to Air Marshal Hugh Pugh Lloyd's staff. Despite all these gruelling operations, he still found time to write at length about those matters that interested him. One of his letters describes a long talk he had with his observer over the intercom during a dusk patrol, on subjects that were not at all what you might expect during a military operation:

March 10th 1943, Algiers: We flew last night on a dusk patrol from 6 to 9 and I quite enjoyed it. The intercom being good, we talked occasionally which is rather unusual and he told about his youth. Apparently his father is one of the elders in the local church and he himself was in charge of the Sunday school of 90 children.

The subject then drifted round to the Divinity and he said that primarily and fundamentally he believed in a Divinity of some sort, though in what form he did not know.

He said that at one time, he had intended to go into the church but gave it up because he couldn't accept so much of the stuff – it would have been hypocrisy to go on.

We agreed that nothing disillusioned a man so much as a war and he said that his best friend came out of the last war after having never been in a church and became a Minister. I think I see what he's getting at. He is realising increasingly that life in the service tends to be futile.

Later in the same letter, Michael wrote:

Of one thing I am sure, you cannot reconcile Christianity to the war. Christ said – 'turn the other cheek', not 'go and bomb them four times as heavily as they bombed you.' Christianity is permeated with the idea of returning good for evil. All we have done is to explain that for the sake of the future, and many other things, we are justified this time in returning evil for evil. Besides this there is the other question of whether you can make up for suffering by inflicting still more and whether you gain anything anyway by adding more chaos to that which already exists.

It is obviously a better thing not to fight unless there is some good reason for it so in our case we are amply justified in doing so. The whole of our future depends on winning the war as does the future of pretty well the whole world. That is justification enough. Now I'm not arguing that the war is either justified or not justified. All I am saying is that in my opinion war is unChristian and that the church ought to say so and not compromise with public opinion.

Like many of his generation, Michael thought a lot about what had to be done after the war and, writing from RAF Church Fenton on 10 September 1941, he said:

The question of what sort of world is going to result from the war is of vital importance to the young people of today. It's going to be their world, their families are going to live in it. Are we going to allow a world to exist where our children are killed as they are here each night?

I wouldn't lift a finger to fight for the British Empire and all the egos it embodies. No anarchist, communist nor even a revolutionary, I am only a Christian who believes that this war will give the world and the Christian forces in it the supreme chance of making a fresh start realising that all men have the right to live and worship their god in their own way. Who can say this way is right, this way is wrong? Religion is very largely a personal interpretation, that one must realise. But oh, to see Christians united on a common ground instead of disunited by petty differences. What people don't understand is that what they think now – every minute – is in a minute way contributing to the sort of post-war world.

Commenting on the Beveridge Report of 1942, Michael wrote from Algiers on 20 March 1943:

Beveridge does not basically solve anything. It seems to me to tackle the problem from the bud and not the root. It says we will construct machinery to deal with cases of want and hardship and poverty as they arise instead of saying we will build a state where, in the main, they don't arise.

I feel the Beveridge report aims at supporting our tottering social system rather than doing what we ought to do and what is the only lasting solution, namely to build a sound social and economic system.

Perhaps it is put on the market by the old capitalist element in order to soothe the people and avoid a change-over which would take the power out of their hands. We must have a complete and radical change in outlook and attitude.

As the last five years have been devoted to destruction and chaos so the next years must be devoted to building and designing and reorganising an order. We will build schools and hospitals, libraries and laboratories, roads and railways, stations and new churches – the whole countryside will show to later generations the change from the spirit of antagonism and destruction to one of co-operation and reconstruction. No more shall the country be run for the benefit of the few but by everyone for the benefit of everyone.

The state must use the talents and skill of the individual for improving the conditions of the community – medical services, travel facilities and back again to schools.

On 30 March 1944, Michael commented on Churchill's attitude and the Cabinet's decision to oppose demands for equal pay for women: 'People are tired of being told what to do as shown by the by-elections and though presumably he will get away with it this time, he won't do so indefinitely.'

His criticisms of the Labour Party were based in part on the fact that it was in the Coalition and, like many people with his views, Michael took an interest in the Common Wealth Party, which, led by Richard Acland, was fighting by-elections on a socialist programme.

At the end of 1943 Michael was posted back to England and began his last tour of duty flying Mosquitoes, taking part in the famous low-level attack on Amiens Prison to liberate the prisoners held there by the Germans.

On 23 June 1944, Michael took off on a mission, but discovered when he was airborne that his air-speed indicator was not working and it would therefore be impossible to complete the mission. He was advised to drop his bombs in the sea, and another plane was asked to come in with him to indicate his air speed as he landed at

RAF Tangmere in Sussex. But he overshot the runway, his plane hit the sea wall and went into the water beyond, and his neck was broken. He died later that day in St Richard's Hospital, Chichester, with my mother at his bedside, who was comforted only by the knowledge that, had he lived, he would have been totally paralysed.

Few, if any, wartime servicemen and women thought of themselves as defending the pre-war world, believing that they were fighting to prevent a return to the unemployment, poverty and militarism of the 1930s. Though Michael did not live to see it, it was those same personal convictions that were later expressed in the establishment of the United Nations and the building of the welfare state, which we then thought were objectives that made all the sacrifices worthwhile.

I greatly loved my brother Michael, and his death was a shattering blow to the whole family. The telegram arrived at the beginning of a class in Rhodesia, where I too was learning to fly. Thinking about his own life and his own ideas, I see him as a young man very much in tune with the aspirations of young people at the beginning of this century, for whom the war is a distant memory of their grandparents, although the ideas of that generation seem fresh and bright and optimistic.

My younger brother David was born when the family was in Scotland, having moved there after the Thames floods had ruined our house in London. He has always been the intellectual in the family, and was known from quite an early age as 'the professor', retaining an interest in high academic standards, which he has put to good use in his own life.

In 1935, David was suddenly taken very seriously ill with TB in his intestines, which had led to a number of lumps developing there, and we all thought he would die. Somehow he pulled through and there is no doubt that his own will power helped. He would never allow anyone to refer to his illness and just said, if asked, that he was 'staying in bed today', showing personal courage that inspired the whole family.

As I have already mentioned it was through his doctor, a Russian immigrant to Britain, that my brother took an interest in the Russian language. He bought Hugo's *Teach Yourself Russian* and learned it by himself, encouraged but not taught by Dr Bromley on his visits. David became so proficient that when he visited the Soviet Union later, he was treated as a native Russian and was even congratulated on his Moscow accent.

When he was sent away to Bexhill and Bournemouth with Nurse Olive, the family was deprived of his company for much of the time, and to some extent the household lost its central focus because Nurse Olive had been removed.

During the first months of his illness, David was taken out for walks in a spinal carriage – a long, flat, high perambulator – and used to go and watch the Changing of the Guard at Horse Guards Parade in Whitehall. The sight of him dressed up in a toy Horse Guard's uniform, gazing up at the Household Cavalry, attracted the attention of a photographer in July 1938 and a picture appeared in a newspaper above the text, 'Although he may never ride a horse, he's as smart as any Guardsman with his shining helmet, breast plate and sword.'

It was not until 1938, at the age of ten, that David was able to stand, and we have a picture of him with his emaciated legs, leaning against the wall outside the guest-house where he was staying in Bexhill; it was a tremendous triumph for him that he had managed to pull through and begin to lead a normal life.

In the summer of 1940, when the Blitz was imminent, a number of children from England were sent to America, and David was very keen that he should not be moved himself, so he wrote to my mother about this from his boarding school in Devon. In his letter he said, 'I would rather be bombed to fragments than leave England now' – a very dramatic way of describing his feelings. My mother wrote anonymously to *The Times* and quoted this letter, believing that the views of the children should be taken into account before they were sent away; Father also wrote to Brendan Bracken, Churchill's Minister of Information:

My dear Brendan

If you want to see the sort of people the PM is leading read the enclosed. I received it entirely unprompted from my youngest. The 'happy childhood' he referred to includes three years on his back. He is as strong as a lion now and recently presented himself to the local ARP office with the demand 'I want a grown up job with some risk'.

Yours Wedgwood Benn

Churchill was so impressed by this that he composed a hand-written letter to my dad:

My dear Benn

A splendid letter from your boy. We must all try to live up to this standard. Thank you for sending it to Brendan.

Every good wish

Yours very sincerely

Winston S. Churchill

Churchill also sent to my brother David a copy of his *My Early Life*. This was in July, just after France had fallen and when an invasion was imminent. It was extraordinary that the Prime Minister found the time to write personally on such a matter.

My brother David replied to thank Churchill, and delivered his letter in person to Number 10 Downing Street, writing: it 'will be interesting in my later life to remember your kindness and to keep your book as a relic for ever'. David was unaware of all the press coverage, because it was thought that it would 'turn his head'. I knew this and, of course, could not resist telling my brother that the publicity had been withheld from him, in case it made him conceited. The correspondence is now in the Churchill archives in Cambridge.

When the communist newspaper, the *Daily Worker*, was banned by the government for its opposition to the war, David – who was living at our uncle's house in Oxted, Surrey – was incensed at the erosion of civil liberties, and bought a little John Bull toy printing set. He carefully prepared a leaflet about three inches square, saying 'Lift the ban on the Daily Worker'. He left it on trains and buses – whether the City gents who travelled from Oxted to London every day were much influenced, I do not know, but it was worth a try.

After the war, David went to Balliol College, became Secretary of the Oxford Union, and practised as a barrister although, looking very youthful, it was not altogether credible to see this mere boy in a wig. In his first case, which was a domestic argument between two neighbours, he appeared for one of them and at the end the judge, in a moment of confusion, bound over 'Mr Benn to keep the peace', instead of the offending neighbour.

After that, being a very good linguist, David went for a time to the Socialist International, and from there joined the BBC

World Service at Bush House, where he eventually became Head of the Yugoslav Service. After he left the BBC, he continued to take a keen interest in Soviet affairs and, among his own archives (for it is a family disease), he has almost every copy of *Pravda* from 1955 in a garage at his house. He makes good use of them as a contributor to the BBC Russian Service and is an active member of the Royal Institute of International Affairs.

Dave has always had a phenomenal memory for dates and details and, when my memory lets me down, I ring him and get the right answer; he is a walking reference book. He has also written a book about Soviet propaganda, pointing out that the absence of democracy makes it difficult for an authoritarian government to know what people really think; as a result, its propaganda ceases to be effective because it is not directed at people's concerns and therefore fails to deal with the underlying problems that face the government. This was, no doubt, one of the factors that led to the collapse of the Soviet Union itself.

He married June, a teacher from Yorkshire; she is a prolific novelist, a keen student of family history and, by dint of this, has discovered that the Benns have deep roots in Yorkshire. This has helped my own son Hilary, now a Leeds MP, to discover that his great-great-great-grandfather was married in a church in Leeds, just a few yards from where he now lives.

David and June have two children: their son is a philosopher who teaches at Imperial College and concentrates on medical ethics; and their daughter, who herself worked for the BBC and has a little boy, Michael.

In 1935 my mother became pregnant with her fourth child and, as it was such a surprise, we nicknamed it 'the Bombshell' and looked forward greatly to its arrival. The birth was due in August, when we were all at Stansgate. Sadly, the pregnancy went wrong. Mother sensed that there was something amiss because one day the baby stopped kicking. But our doctor (who, we later heard, had been a drug addict) did not arrange an immediate Caesarian and, when Jeremy was born, he was dead. The doctor took the little body away in a white metal container, leaving us to grieve. My mother never forgot Jeremy and, more than ten years later, my father was determined to find the baby's body so that he could be given a proper funeral.

He went to immense trouble and finally located the woman who had worked in the doctor's surgery in Burnham. She remembered the incident and the fact that the baby had been buried in the same white container in an unconsecrated part of a cemetery. My dad located it, managed to get an exhumation order from a local magistrate so that the body could be lifted; then another certificate allowed a cremation, and the baby's ashes were interred in a small church, where my elder brother Michael's ashes had been laid and where my father's and mother's ashes are now buried.

This simple act gave my mother immense happiness and provided us all as a family with a chance to pay tribute to the baby brother we had never seen.

6

How I Became a Philistine!

During my childhood and growing up, no attempt was made to develop the artistic, musical and literary side of life, and that became a serious disadvantage as I got older.

My mother read a lot of theological books, and my dad scanned *The Times* and filed it for future reference, but neither encouraged me to read. I was taken to the theatre only once or twice and, because I was no good at music, my music teachers at school took no interest in me, which denied me the opportunity of developing my tastes. I have described how as a child I never visited the Tate Gallery, though our house was right next door.

The one exception (though a limited one) in my cultural education was my enjoyment of films, and I do recall with enormous pleasure some of the classics that I saw as a youngster, and which I still love to watch.

One was *The Life and Death of Colonel Blimp*, which I must have seen when it first came out during the war, and which I have watched many times since on video. That film excited me in part because of its historical span, from the Boer War through the First World War into the Second. But I loved also the figure of Colonel Blimp himself, whom Low the cartoonist had invented as a figure of fun but who, in the film, was developed into a man whose convictions were rooted in experience and who, though apparently so intransigent and arrogant at the end of his life, had a very human side to him. The film had depth and understanding, including its sympathetic portrayal of the position of a German officer, which led Churchill to believe that it might undermine the war effort and at one stage to contemplate a ban on it.

Another film that I saw at about the same time was *Proud Valley*, with Paul Robeson as a black American miner trying to get a job in a South Wales colliery. Initially finding himself rejected on the grounds that he was black (the objection coming from miners who were themselves black with coal dust) he was then welcomed into the miners' ranks – a welcome that was especially warm because he was a brilliant singer who gave their choir phenomenal strength. In the film, Robeson joined with his Welsh comrades in a march on London to save a colliery, and some compromise was reached with the coal owners – a rather weak ending, which I later learned was enforced on the film-maker because the original was considered too radical for wartime.

Paul was the son of a slave. He threw himself into socialist and peace campaigns in a way that led to his denunciation as a fellow-traveller during the Cold War. I met him in London in 1958 when the Americans had restored his passport and he was able to travel. He said that when he went to Wales, he realised two things: firstly, that he was an African, and secondly, that he was a member of the working class.

Another wartime film was *The Way to the Stars*, which was based on the experience of Halfpenny Field, an airfield once occupied by the RAF and then taken over by the Americans when they came into the war; the relationship between the air crew and the local pub, where Rosamund John played the manager, was very skilfully directed. Michael Redgrave played the British pilot who fell in love with Rosamund John, and who was subsequently killed in action.

When Redgrave's character died, he left behind a poem, written by John Pudney, called 'For Johnny Head-in-Air'. And when the Member of Parliament Bob Cryer was killed in 1994, I was asked to read that poem at his graveside, standing facing Bob's widow and children, before his body was lowered into the grave.

The Way to the Stars exactly captured the mood of the RAF and I find the film very nostalgic, having been stationed at Moreton-in-Marsh once as an air cadet.

Similarly, A Matter of Life and Death caught the same spirit, with David Niven almost dying in an air crash but being found alive, after he had baled out on a beach, by an American girl and falling in love. The story was a battle between Heaven and Earth as to who should have him. It was dramatic and powerful. The prosecutor in heaven was an American from the revolutionary war, and the court was made up of thousands of British and American soldiers who had died; the film had a considerable audience in the United States.

I also loved Brief Encounter, the story of a suburban housewife who fell for a doctor she met on a weekly visit to a local town; although he only kissed her, he recognised the danger of what lay ahead and felt that he should emigrate to Africa to avoid breaking up their respective marriages. The film ended with a tragic farewell in a station buffet, as the doctor left to catch the train and she went home to her husband – and all was well, according to the morality of the time.

I am at heart a very sentimental person, easily moved to tears. In the film *The Railway Children*, when their daddy had been falsely arrested for espionage and finally returned home, and Jenny Agutter stood at the railway station and recognised her father through the steam of the railway engine, I always burst into tears. Indeed, my children describe these moments as 'Railway Children' moments. And when I burst into tears after introducing my son Hilary to the Chamber of the House of Commons in 1999, the family, who were all sitting in the gallery, turned to each other and nodded, whispering, 'It's the Railway Children again.'

Brassed Off! also always makes me cry, being the only authentic drama about the miners' strike of 1984–5, which brings out in a most powerful way the sufferings of the miners and the way they responded with courage and goodwill. It was illuminated by the playing of Rodrigo's 'Orange Juice' (Aranjuez) by the girl who had been a miner's daughter and went to join the colliery band in the village where they were struggling to survive; and it culminated with Pete Postlethwaite as the conductor who, when the band won the contest at the Royal Albert Hall, made a passionate speech rejecting the prize. It all ended happily when the band seized the trophy anyway.

I always cry at the Durham Miners' Gala, standing on the balcony at the County Hotel as the bands go by and the children dance, and the injured miners wave from their wheelchairs as they are pushed past. *Gresford*, written to commemorate a terrible mining disaster, is another real tear-jerker.

I like happy endings and detest violent films, which frighten me and seem designed to acclimatise people to violence, spread despair among the viewers, in exaggerating the evil side of mankind, and encourage hopelessness and cynicism.

High Noon, which had a violent end to it, depicted Gary Cooper as the sheriff married to a woman (Grace Kelly) whose pacifist – probably Quaker – convictions were tested when gangsters came to town to kill him. She saved her husband, resolving the dilemma we would all face in a similar situation.

Another powerful film is *Dr Strangelove*, in which Peter Sellers plays three parts: a German scientist; an RAF officer who is a bit of a buffoon; and the President of the United States, who finds himself sucked into a nuclear incident that he hadn't planned, but which could well have led to a Third World War. Mockery is a powerful instrument in politics and, after watching *Dr Strangelove*, no one could take the case for nuclear weapons seriously.

All my life I have lived in the oral tradition, learning from listening and watching rather than from reading, and communicating by speaking rather than writing. I am not – nor do I aspire to be – an intellectual.

In some ways, however, I do feel the disapproval of intellectuals who look down on people who have lived in the oral tradition; but it is a fact that from a speech you get a multi-dimensional understanding of a person that is not available through the printed word, however beautifully crafted. When you listen to someone, you can make up your mind about the nature of the person speaking and whether they believe in what they are saying. I have learned most of what I know (not least at my surgeries as a Member of Parliament) through listening to people, not from reading books.

Experience comes into play, of course, because with experience you are able to judge the truth of even the most powerful demagogue's speech more directly and personally than if you had read the same words in a book or an article.

The oral tradition is in fact far stronger in history than the written tradition. For generations, people learned by the stories that were told and passed on orally; these made an impact that was greater, it could be argued, than that of written works by clerks and scholars.

I suspect that, in my mind, the Protestant work ethic made the enjoyment of *anything* suspect – that applied equally to reading, and I have undoubtedly denied myself a lot of pleasure by not reading fiction. However, there is also the hard work involved in decoding twenty-six letters before you can understand what the author is saying! I remember at one of the great universities in Beijing someone explained to me that in Chinese the little pictures give greater freedom to your imagination and allow you to visualise, say, a man or a horse. I much favoured that way of communication!

By contrast, my grandchildren are immensely musical and artistic, and when I hear them play or sing I feel most inadequate.

7

The Outbreak of War

We were on holiday at Stansgate in summer 1939 when Hitler invaded Poland. Parliament was recalled, and my parents went back to London. My brothers and I stayed at Stansgate and sat listening to the radio as Chamberlain announced that 'a state of war now exists'. I shall never forget the realisation that this would fundamentally change our lives. I was both relieved and frightened and I sensed that my brother Michael, who was then just eighteen, would volunteer for the Air Force before his call-up papers arrived. Two days later we heard of the first air attack by the RAF on Germany; this was later made into a film called *The Lion Has Wings*, part of the propaganda of war.

I have described how war affected my schooling, with Westminster School being evacuated first to Lancing College in Sussex and then to Exeter University. In 1940 Father was the Member of Parliament for Gorton (Manchester) and he and a number of other MPs joined, or rejoined, the forces. He was sixty-three. My mother was left to look after the constituency as best she could.

I had a telegram from Father and all it said was:

+ I HAVE A NEW JOB. NO RISK. HONOUR BRIGHT! +

At the end of July 1940 the school authorities decided, incredibly, that it was safe to return to Westminster and preparations were made just as the Battle of Britain was beginning! When the Blitz started, the family was living at Millbank. Every night when the siren went off we would hurry to the basement in Thames House just by Lambeth Bridge (now occupied by MI5) and unroll our mats to sleep. Down there was a friendly atmosphere and we got to know everybody well. We could hear the bombing quite clearly, and on one occasion an old lady whom we knew was late in arriving and we were worried. As she came into the shelter we asked, 'What is it like up there?' And she replied, 'It's awful, look at my umbrella, it's absolutely soaked!'

On another occasion a landmine was dropped near the shelter and 500 people were killed in and around Thames House. St John's Westminster, which I had attended as a child every Sunday, was bombed. Coming up in the morning, you could see the fires still blazing over East London, where the docks had been hit, and there were some daylight raids, where I saw the bombers of the Luftwaffe being attacked by anti-aircraft fire.

At that time there was a severe blackout, and every light had to be turned off and the curtains tightly drawn, in the hope that this would make it harder for the bombers to know where they were. Therefore, before we left the house every night we turned off the lights at the mains, but when we returned we found that the electric clocks had moved forward. That summer we had a cook, and we discovered that although she came to the shelter with us, she used to go back to the house and turn on the lights, and we began to suspect that she was a spy.

Father's first reaction was to say, 'It certainly saves money if Hitler pays our cook!' But he did report it to the security services, who duly investigated. When a bomb hit a government department, the record of spies was destroyed and by then our cook had moved elsewhere.

'Digging for Victory' was the current slogan and the need to grow our own food to survive the blockade on imports by German U-boats was very real.

At the height of the Blitz, David and I were moved to Oban, where we stayed at the Columba Hotel; my grandmother and grandfather were also staying there. As soon as I arrived I volunteered for the local Air Raid Precaution (ARP) unit and explained that I had been in London during the Blitz – this was designed to impress them, and did! They were busy preparing for a war that had not yet hit Oban, so my experiences (even though I was only fifteen) were considered quite interesting. Oban was in fact the base for the Sunderland Flying boats, manned by the RAF and crew from the Royal Australian Air Force, who stayed in the hotel, so it could have been a target.

A Warden's Report Form from October that year, in my writing, describes: 'House collapsed and FIRE spreading, THREE German aircraft seen, SIX of ours in pursuit. RAF Motorboats in attendance. Warden SMITH slightly wounded', which must have been a practice report, as there were no raids as far as I remember.

I later received from the Assistant Medical Officer of Argyll County Council a letter thanking me for 'attending so enthusiastically at the First Aid Post'. I wore an armband and I still have my St John Ambulance first-aid manual from that time, full of terribly dangerous advice, including that if someone has a shock, give them a hot drink! I was clearly a precocious fifteen-year-old participant of the civilian preparations for war.

We were in effect refugees and it was very boring, much of the time. One day I clambered out of the window and climbed on to the huge, six-foot-tall letters that spelt out 'Columba Hotel'; I was seen moving from letter to letter and was hauled in. Another day I tried to make gunpowder by getting saltpetre from the chemist, but having completed the mixture, a match failed to ignite it, so I put it on a fire to see if it would burn. It put the fire out.

My brother David, then aged eleven, got so depressed and angry at being sent to safety out of London that he told me he wanted to commit suicide. So I dug out some strong throat lozenges, which burned when you sucked them, and gave him two of them to eat. He then told me that he had changed his mind, and could I help? So I said I had an antidote and gave him four more of the same lozenges. He survived. But I got into a lot of trouble when this was reported. My brother says that when I was bored I could create discord and annoy people and would 'argue the hind leg off a donkey' about anything.

Returning south, I found that the school had been evacuated again, to Buckenhill near Bromyard in Herefordshire, where we took over a series of old buildings, including a Victorian castle called Saltmarsh where all sports were replaced by gardening. We had military exercises and were kitted out in battle-dress, tin hats and gas masks. It was at the age of about sixteen that I first learned how to fire a rifle, do bayonet drill, toss grenades and take part in live-ammunition exercises. They were much more risky than was ever admitted.

The old grenades that we used had a pin in them and, when

you removed the pin, the grenade was safe while you held it because it had a little handle that you gripped. When the handle was released, the grenade went off after five seconds. We were told that under certain circumstances, if you threw a grenade at an enemy soldier, he might catch it and throw it back within five seconds and blow you up instead. The way of dealing with that was to allow the handle to be released, count three and then throw the grenade, so that it exploded just as it dropped into enemy lines. There was one boy who accidentally dropped the grenade just before he threw it, but happily he got behind the sandbag, thus saving himself from death. Where live ammunition is used, the timing has to be very precise and our cadets, working by the clock, had to move out of the positions they occupied before the real bullets were fired at them.

On one occasion the local butcher, who was in the Home Guard and was responsible for a Lewis machine gun, arrived late with his crew and opened fire before the legs of the Lewis gun had been anchored into the ground, so that when he started firing, the bullets went all over the place and we had to run to escape them.

Another time, a 'sticky bomb', which was an anti-tank grenade covered with glue, which you had to take up and attach to the side of an enemy tank, failed to go off. One of the teachers, Mr Murray Rust, had to be sent in to explode this sticky bomb, which as far as I remember he did by firing at it with a pistol.

We were also present at one of the earliest demonstrations of the Blacker Bombard – a thick piece of piping mounted on a stand, at the bottom of which there was a sharp pin. Elementary mortars were dropped into the tube and, as they fell, they struck the pin, which exploded them and fired them off in the general direction of the enemy. There was no serious aiming mechanism and the main thing was to get your head out of the way after you had dropped the bombard into the firing tube. We also used Sten guns, which were all-metal sub-machine guns that got very hot when you fired them. What you had to do was dip them in a bucket of cold water until they cooled off and could be used again.

In Oxted, while still living at Blunt House in school holidays, I had joined the Home Guard and we had a guard room in the village where we gathered every night, preparing for our patrols in case German parachutists arrived. By then some of our rifles had been taken away as they were needed in the Soviet Union, and we were equipped with bayonets stuck in a piece of metal tubing, known as pikes.

At nights I would patrol with my pike and was warned that German parachutists might arrive disguised as nuns – in retrospect, I am glad I never saw a nun, because at sixteen, with a pike and clear instructions to kill on sight, I fear I could have done a lot of damage. In the guard room we did our drill with rifles and were taught how to load them, press our fingers down to keep the top bullet out of the barrel, pushing the bolt over to hold it down, and then press the trigger, leaving the rifle ready to use by pulling the bolt back and pushing it forward. One of the old boys, who had been a general (possibly in the Boer War) and had rejoined the Home Guard, had just been appointed a corporal and was very proud of his stripes. When loading his rifle he followed the instructions, but accidentally pulled the bolt back twice, so the gun was loaded; he fired a bullet through the wall, which passed through the lavatory of the house next door, which a woman was using at the time.

Indignantly she banged at the guard-room door and shouted, 'You are not to be trusted with guns.' Quivering, we kept the door locked until the inspecting officer for the area called later that night. When we reported the incident to him, he said it was the third he had heard about that evening.

It seemed fun at the time. But a complete generation of young men was being taught how to kill, and believed that it was necessary to do so, to keep the enemy out of Britain. In retrospect, I think that was quite an influence in shaping people's attitudes to violence and death. It certainly contributed to my own continuing detestation of war.

My father and my brother Michael had both joined the RAF in 1940; I enlisted two years later when I was seventeen, but was not called up until the summer of 1943. By then I had been at Oxford for a year studying – in a desultory way – for a philosophy, politics and economics degree, but expecting at any moment to go off to war.

8

From Oxford to the RAF

When I left Westminster School to go to New College, Oxford, it was a leap to freedom, with the opportunity to plan my own time away from the disciplines of school. It was of course short-lived, but I enjoyed it enormously. I cannot recall the reason why I went to that college, or how much my parents paid in fees. The academic side of university never interfered with my political and social life.

It was at New College that I met David Butler, who became a close friend, and we went together to tutorials with Philip Andrews, who taught us economics and smoked a pipe (as did his wife). He probably influenced me to take up a pipe myself, and it has been a great source of comfort to me ever since.

In 1943 the university was totally different to the pre-war Oxford and to the Oxford of today, because we were all waiting to go into the services. I myself spent a lot of time with the Air Squadron, where we did some basic training prior to joining up.

But even in the normal life of the university at the Oxford

Union, in which I was very active, the war dominated the debates because we were all thinking about what sort of a world we wanted when it was over, and discussing issues that were to arise in the election of 1945.

Indeed, I made my 'maiden speech' in the Oxford Union on the Beveridge Report. The *Oxford Magazine* account of the debate stated that I 'showed the wider implications of the motion, which made even the Beveridge Report itself seem irrelevant'. Later, another motion proposed that 'planning social security would involve the loss of liberty'. It was defeated by 128 to 89 votes. Frank Pakenham (Lord Longford) and Geoffrey Rippon also participated in the debate.

On 4 March 1943, Richard Acland spoke on the motion 'that in the opinion of this house reconstruction in Europe and in Britain is impossible unless all the major productive resources entirely cease to be owned by private individuals'. It was carried by the casting vote of the President.

In my speech I said that it involved the fundamental issue of capitalism versus socialism. Tony Crosland, who was back on leave from the army, 'ably endeavoured to refute the argument that work is less well done by the state's employ than the capitalist's, though admitting he found himself in uneasy partnership with Dick Acland'.

Later in May there was a debate on the motion 'that the state should design and build the Englishman's castle' – an argument for a huge public housing programme, which I moved with some passion. The *Oxford Magazine* commented that 'The mover was confident and handled his arguments well but he must avoid treating the house as a class or a Salvation Army meeting'! My motion was defeated by 58 to 46 votes.

I also threw myself with great enthusiasm into the Oxford University Labour Party Association and was elected to the executive committee at a time when A. D. Lindsay of Balliol was the President and Patrick Gordon Walker was Senior Treasurer. At our meetings we discussed local government, the Labour Party, the trade-union movement, education and the role of women in politics.

Most of my friends would gather in the evening to discuss the post-war world. We were frequently interrupted by practice air-raid exercises, and on one occasion one of the dons came to my room and announced that a bomb had landed nearby; he had to tie a label round my leg, stating 'Severe burns'. A bucket full of paper had been lit to make the exercise realistic, but had gone out before the fire brigade arrived to extinguish it. I told him that I had a lot of work to do, so he agreed to change the label to say 'Slight burns', to avoid my being carried off to casualty!

All that came to an end in the summer of 1943 when I joined the RAF as an Aircraftsman Second Class (AC2), and was kitted up, put in a block of flats in St John's Wood and found myself at the London Zoo, where our meals were served. We were eventually posted to the Initial Training Wing at Stratford-upon-Avon, where we were put up in a series of requisitioned hotels as air cadets.

It was all very easy-going and I remember on one occasion there was terrible trouble because some of the cadets, having had a drop too much to drink, went out with paintbrushes and, wherever the word 'Shakespeare' appeared, painted 'Bacon' – who was believed by some scholars (including the late Enoch Powell) to have been the true author. The anger of the residents of Stratford-upon-Avon when they saw their beautiful theatre daubed 'Bacon Memorial

Theatre' knew no bounds, and the offenders were severely disciplined by officers who, even if they were quietly laughing, had to hide their amusement in order to retain their reputation with the locals.

From there I was stationed at RAF Elmdon, which was the municipal airport of Birmingham. This was where I began my flying training on Tiger Moths, whose design came straight out of the Biggles period of the First World War. It was a wooden biplane with two open cockpits and we sat on our parachutes. We wore goggles and a leather jacket and helmet and communicated between the two cockpits by means of a rubber speaking-tube, through which you were just audible above the noise of the engine.

Living in Nissen huts, we would get up about five o'clock, have breakfast (which consisted of a bun and a cup of steaming cocoa, so thick that you could stand a spoon up in it) and go into the hangar, where a couple of us would drag a Tiger Moth out onto the tarmac. As we clambered into our cockpits and did our basic drill, someone would put wooden chocks under the wheels, catch hold of the propeller with one hand, and we would shout 'Contact' as we switched on the engine; the man would then swing the propeller until it started like a powered lawnmower. We would shout 'Chocks away', open the throttle and taxi out for take-off, to do our 'circuits and bumps' – which was the way we described the initial training, made up of a succession of take-offs, circuits of the airfield and bumpy landings. None of us flew solo at Elmdon, but we were tested for our suitability and then posted to Heaton Park in Manchester, waiting to go abroad for our proper training.

I could hardly believe my luck that I was being paid two shillings a day to have such a happy time. Among our amusements was flying low over a nearby nudist camp, where we saw the naturists running for cover as we zoomed over them, waving at anyone who seemed to be friendly. A few years ago I had a letter from a man who remembered living as a boy near Elmdon and how thrilled he was to see these planes flying over.

It was very dangerous learning to fly in Britain, where we would have been a sitting target for enemy fighters. They would have shot us down in our hundreds, so we did our real training abroad.

I got to Heaton Park in Manchester in the autumn of 1943. It had been a huge public open space and a lake, but now it was covered with Nissen huts where we nearly froze to death; we had one little coke-fired boiler in the middle, which we were not allowed to light until evening and which had gone out by morning. We walked to do our ablutions in another ice-cold building and ate our meals in a large hall. There was nothing whatsoever for us to do, as we were waiting for a troop ship to take us to do our training in South Africa, Canada or America.

We were mainly sent on long and exhausting route marches to keep us busy. At one stage my job was to be posted to the edge of Heaton Park, to stop RAF men from jumping over the wall and going into Manchester for a night off. It was quite a cushy job because there was such confusion that it was easy to jump over the wall myself and have an evening out in Manchester with my mates. One very foggy night I had just done this when, out of the fog, I could see a route march approaching, headed by a very big sergeant. I only just managed to slip into the fog myself before I was spotted.

In January 1944 we were issued with tropical gear and sent on a train to Glasgow, to be embarked on the *Cameronia*, which set sail on 11 January and went through the Straits of Gibraltar and the Mediterranean to Egypt, then via the Suez Canal down to

Durban. Going through the Suez Canal into the Red Sea, we saw the Italian fleet, which had surrendered, moored in the Bitter Lakes.

The conditions on the ship were not too grand, since we were sitting along tables facing each other for long stretches; at night we slung hammocks above them or found somewhere to sleep on deck on the long voyage to Durban. The U-boats were active as we came down past Spain and we heard depth-charges being dropped, which were like hammer blows on the sides of the ship. As we were below the water line, it was slightly nerve-racking, but we got across the Mediterranean safely and through the Suez Canal.

Once, the troopship got stuck in the mud on the Canal and the captain had the brilliant idea of using the Tannoy to tell us all to go to the other side of the ship; he shouted, 'One, two, three, jump!', which we did, and the ship freed itself and we carried on.

Life on board was incredibly boring, but we made up for it by talking all the time, and on one occasion we decided to have a meeting about war aims. I was deputed to go and ask the Officer Commanding Troops, so I went to his cabin, saluted sharply and sought his approval.

'There would be no politics in it, would there?' asked the colonel, so I saluted again and said, 'No, sir.' And we then had the most lively debate about the post-war world and how it should be organised. Of course the body of men came from a much wider social background than I was used to, so my real political education began in the RAF and developed more fully when, after the war, my formal education ended.

We took on board some Italian prisoners en route to a prisoner-of-war camp and these wretched men were confined in the depths of the ship. One of them died on board and we had a funeral at sea, with proper military honours: his body was thrown overboard in a canvas sack with a weight attached to it, though we all knew that it would probably be eaten by sharks long before it got to the bottom of the sea. I found that a very painful experience as I thought of his family. I assumed that he, like many Italians, had suffered under Mussolini and had been conscripted into the forces.

We landed at Durban and it was like going back to the pre-war world; I remember seeing a banana for the first time since 1939. We were put in a transit camp waiting for a long train journey north to Rhodesia, where I was to complete my training. I had twenty-four hours free to visit my aunt, who lived in Pietermaritzburg. Then it was back to the camp and on to the train, north to Bulawayo in Southern Rhodesia.

It was a fabulous journey, and the end of each carriage had an open platform on which you could sit and watch the sun go down; as we climbed the mountains, the train went so slowly that you could jump off and walk, then jump on again before it gathered speed. After three days we got to Bulawayo and were sent to Hillside Camp, another transit camp, where we were to stay until we went on to our flying school.

Wearing shorts and a bush jacket with a topi, we looked like early colonial settlers; indeed, that was the atmosphere in Rhodesia at that time. We went into Bulawayo for the evening, and I have recounted elsewhere my failed attempt to strike up a friendship with Gloria, who worked in a hairdresser's shop and spent the evening serving meals to us in the Services Club. I blushed so scarlet when I spoke to her that she asked me if I would like a cold drink; deeply embarrassed, I fled.

We also met Ginyilitshe, an old Matabele warrior who had fought with Lobengula against Cecil Rhodes, and who came and described the battle. I was kindly welcomed into the home of the Aulds, whose daughter Mary Fletcher was a nurse. She took me to the local hospital for Africans, where the conditions were appalling. I have kept in touch with Mary, who came to see me recently. I also phoned Gloria, just before she died two years ago.

During my time in Rhodesia 60,000 whites were in total control, living off the land that had been stolen from the Matebele and the Mashona by Rhodes, with the Africans having no vote at all. That experience first interested me in the anti-colonial movement, and became my main interest when I was elected to Parliament. It has made me appreciate why Britain is the last country in the world to be entitled to lecture Mugabe, the dictator of Zimbabwe, on the importance of democracy and human rights.

My diaries *Years of Hope* record my life in Africa, my training as a pilot, the death of my brother while I was there, and the trip on to Egypt, where the war in Europe ended just after I had got my wings.

9

Caroline

I arrived home in a troopship in time to play some part in the election campaign of July 1945 and returned to Oxford to complete my degree. I had transferred to the Fleet Air Arm in the hope that I might serve in the Far East, but that plan collapsed with the end of the Japanese war following the atomic bombing of Hiroshima and Nagasaki. As I was no longer needed, I was released.

Post-war Oxford was of course by then full of ex-servicemen who had seen action. It was a telescoped generation, with students who had been colonels, including a man in his mid-twenties who had been blinded and lost a leg.

David Butler had been in a tank that sank while crossing the Rhine, and Tony Crosland was back from the army, finishing his degree and acting as a tutor as well – known as a pseudo-don. He too became a firm friend.

I was there from 1946 to 1948, and it was in Crosland's rooms in 1947 that I met Hugh Dalton, who had just been sacked for leaking his Budget to a journalist as he entered the House to deliver it. I accidentally greeted him as Chancellor, to which he boomed, 'No, the ex-Chancellor.'

Dalton was talking to some philosophy students about the books they read, and they discussed their work with him. Then he mentioned a German name that I had never heard of. It silenced them. They looked at each other in embarrassment, and I suspected that he had made up the name to see how they would react. But I dared not ask him if it was a joke. That was typical of Dalton.

I was elected President of the Oxford Union and was chosen to lead a debating tour with Edward Boyle and Kenneth Harris to the United States in the autumn of 1947–8. We visited sixty colleges and universities in forty-two states and discussed a number of contemporary issues, including a motion favouring an Anglo-American alliance. While there I met a number of American students, one of whom, T. George Harris, later introduced me to Caroline DeCamp in the summer of 1948 when she visited Oxford from Vassar College to attend a summer school.

We met on 2 August, saw each other every day and nine days later, on 11 August, sitting on a bench in a churchyard in Oxford on the eve of her departure for America, I realised that I would never see her again. When I first met Caroline I was not immediately struck by her and had no idea that within just over a week I would have proposed to her.

She accepted, and so began the most important relationship of my life, for she and our children, Stephen, Hilary, Melissa and Joshua, had by far the greatest influence on me. The bench, which I later bought for £10, was in our front garden for fifty years until it was moved to Stansgate and placed by the grave where her ashes are now buried in the garden.

It was at about this time that I had a strange invitation to take up a government job. My old headmaster approached me and said he had heard of a post that I might be interested in, but he couldn't tell me what it was. However, he could arrange for me to meet the person concerned.

Partly out of curiosity and partly because I would need a job once married, I agreed to meet a Colonel Sheridan, who asked me if I would be interested in working indirectly for the Foreign Office at a salary of £1,000 a year – which was more than twice the salary I had at the BBC the following year. I thanked him for the suggestion, but said that I hoped one day to be elected to Parliament and that MPs were not allowed to take government jobs (known as 'offices of profit under the Crown'), which disqualify the holders from election.

'Oh,' he said, 'that's no problem; you could do both jobs as an MP, if elected, and there is no cause to worry on that account.'

At that stage I had a word with my dad, because I was very suspicious. He said, 'Don't touch it with a barge pole' and made it clear that he believed (as I had guessed) that it was a job with the security services.

So I wrote back to Colonel Sheridan on 13 December 1948:

> After a great deal of thought I have decided not to send my name forward for the job we discussed on Friday. The real difficulty arises from what seems to me an almost inescapable incompatibility between the work you spoke of and my political activities.

But that was not the end of Colonel Sheridan, because even after I had been elected to the House of Commons, he came to see me and in effect asked me to do the same job.

It was only after his death that I realised that the appointment he had in mind was in the IRD, a part of the security services set up by Chris Mayhew during the Cold War. When he died, Sheridan's obituary described his real role (and the role of IRD and its links with MI6), which was to write anti-communist stories and have them planted in the press. For the Cold War had begun as soon as the Second World War ended, and from then until the fall of the Berlin Wall it was the main preoccupation of the security services.

I was shocked, and remain shocked, at the thought that the security services should have been able to defy the constitution and employ elected MPs as spies for them, on the basis that this would never be publicly disclosed. I later came to believe that there were MPs who were doing just that, and no doubt still are. The fact that such an offer was explicitly made to me means that this suspicion is not a conspiracy theory, but founded on a real event.

Moreover, I assume they approached me because, as the son of a peer, a public-school boy, an Oxford graduate and a former RAF pilot, I would be considered on class grounds to be reliable, since class has always been the basis for a presumption of loyalty to the Crown and the basis of recruitment to positions in the security services. It also showed that they knew nothing about my politics, for if they had made the most elementary enquiries, they would have discovered that I was a socialist who was committed to the very policies that the security services would have regarded as fundamentally disloyal. But then the intelligence services have never been very bright.

After Caroline returned to America and before I went over for the wedding the next year, she and I discovered, during a long and detailed correspondence, that we had many shared beliefs and experiences that had shaped our thinking in childhood. In one of her letters she wrote:

As far as American politics go, and that is all I know, having never studied the subject elsewhere, I have always been torn between the existing parties and practices and never really wholeheartedly devoted myself to any particular one. This is especially true of the present situation which climaxes in the coming election.

I was violently in favor of Roosevelt much against my family's views, for they have always been Republican; but I was quite young and vastly disinterested in the subject during most of the time he was in office. So I guess my sympathies were mostly with his ideals and what I fancied he stood for and was driving towards, rather than with the specific practices and acts he was responsible for. But then in this field my reasoning is highly likely to be based on idealistic rather than practical grounds.

I think the machinery of democratic government available to both our countries a remarkable and useable system. But unfortunately in this country anyway an honorable set of ideals and a desirable theory doesn't always ensure a sound practice. The Bossism, the lack of interest in political affairs and the niggling stupidity of a great many of our political leaders has always made me cringe; and for a long time I was so discouraged that I refused to even think about it at all . . .

Caroline voted for Henry Wallace in 1948 and wrote:

In a way I don't blame the Wallace people . . . for sticking to the basic Marxian idea of revolution. Because things are pretty hopeless. Yet even the fact that the changes here are so remote does not justify such a code to me, especially in view of the fact that the basic desirable changes can be brought about peacefully. And yet as I have said, I have much sympathy with them because they are willing to do something and have energies and capacities that are outstanding and because, in general, their ends are noble and that always appeals to me.

She also wrote at length about religion and described how her family were Anglicans and were given the usual childhood religious training, but none of them was passionately devout. It was only when she went to school:

. . . where with the strict sequestered life we led and the fact that we had to go to chapel twice daily, things of this nature began to assume an importance hitherto unknown. I became violently religious and acutely conscious of the fact that my own life was unbelievably below the Christian ethical standards.

I did everything in my power to obey to the letter. Naturally this couldn't be done and for a while I developed something of the Christian guilt complex which I see so strongly in your letters. I was really miserable and for a while quite gave up hope for my small soul. But then, with graduating, living at the naval air station and entering college I became involved in outside activities and goals and the Christian scale of right and wrong began to be tempered by the human scale of such.

And there is that distinction, because the Christian ethics, if interpreted as I had done, are really inhuman, and it is only the saints and martyrs who can hope to keep them.

There is a great similarity between the ethical codes of all religions. They all preach tolerance, the golden rule, peace and honesty.

Of course there are differences but I still maintain that they are not of such a vital nature that they cannot be reconciled with one another . . .

I believe from the bottom of my heart that religion is a human as much as a divine problem.

I believe that it is after all only a divine myth, much like all other myths that have been invented by various civilisations and peoples, to explain that which is mysterious and to provide laws for societies which demand them by their own incompetence to handle life decently.

Ritual has very powerful effects over me but they are not any the less simply because I believe they are just ritual and not a divine ordination handed down from heaven.

What does constitute heaven I do not know.

We are human beings and as such are completely incapable of understanding things divine. The most we can do is to have faith which I do have and have very strongly and make the best of what has been given to us – our lives.

In retrospect, perhaps the most significant passage in one of Caroline's letters was about her love of the arts. I wish I had reread it regularly, for it was an important aspect of her life, which I was unable to share but which explained so much about her:

My real loves are the arts and I just can't help it. One Beethoven trio is worth a hundred presidential elections to me and I cannot look at it otherwise. I will try to be interested in the things you are because I do want to know about them and because I do not want to let you down in any way, but the key to the world to me lies in literature and music and philosophy, and that is the only route I can ever take to really discover what this life is all about. Even if I don't particularly care for someone in a great way, if they are lifted out of a day by a Scarlatti sonata or discovering themselves in a Thomas Mann character I warm up to them in the most immediate way.

The kinship I feel with all the university people I am with this Fall, is entirely based on the fact that our interests in life, our real interests, are precisely the same. We are violently different as people but we all feel unconsciously that the really important things in life are the same; and although our ideas and opinions differ greatly, the sense of togetherness these common interests create is fantastic. When I am in a group or a place where no-one thinks much on the things I do, or where the things that matter are so entirely in a different field of study, I begin to think how narrow and unimportant are my tastes and likes.

I just will never be able to find anything that is of such supreme interest and importance to me, so maybe I should just stop worrying about it.

Caroline was born in Cincinnati, Ohio, a descendant of a family of Huguenots who had originally come to America to escape from repression in France in the seventeenth century. In 1812 Ezekiel and Mary Baker DeCamp, her immediate forebears, with ten of their children, took a journey that lasted six days in a covered waggon, pulled by horse and oxen, from New Jersey to settle in Ohio. There a further seven children were born, all but one (Moses, who died at ten) living to adult life.

Within less than one hundred years of their marriage, they had more than 700 descendants by 1896, and a later updated history edited by Caroline's brother Graydon in 1976 lists twelve generations, from the first DeCamps who had come from France nearly 300 years before and whose descendants must now run into tens of thousands.

The early DeCamps were dedicated Christians – Methodists and Presbyterians, hard-working and God-fearing, who worked as stonemasons, bricklayers, carpenters and plasterers, some founding businesses and with a strong sense of their public duty. Six of the DeCamp brothers were introduced to President Lincoln, a few months before his assassination, and he was told that they had all voted for him and prayed every day for him to receive divine guidance.

Caroline's mother was a Graydon, of Protestant Irish stock, who, as Caroline once said to me, had waited for the Pullman cars to be running before they came to Ohio – her grandfather being a Chaucer scholar and a partner in a law firm in Cincinnati.

I do not think Caroline's Republican parents ever quite understood the radical ideas that she had formed for herself – not least her voting for Henry Wallace in the presidential election of 1948, at a time when he was receiving support from socialists and communists.

Caroline was brought up, as I was, as an Anglican. But she became a humanist, as I have done, cherishing the rituals of the Church, but unable to subscribe to the Creed, while embracing the moral teachings of the Bible, believing them best realised in collective political and social action.

At Vassar College, where she graduated with distinction, she organised a Radical Arts Conference to bring arts and society together; because of its success, it finally won round the support of the authorities who had initially disapproved of it.

From there, and after our engagement, she went on to do a

graduate degree at the University of Cincinnati with a thesis on Milton, and when we arrived in London she did a second graduate degree at University College, with a thesis on Stuart Masques and the co-operation between Ben Jonson and Inigo Jones.

In January 1949 I went by boat to New York, where Caroline was waiting, and on by train to Cincinnati to meet her family. They could not have been nicer, considering that they knew nothing about me, other than what Caroline had told them. They arranged a party at their home to meet their wider family, and I was taken to Caroline's grandfather's house for Sunday lunch, in a huge 'Elizabethan' building that they had put up in the 1930s, with a library full of books, including some of his about Geoffrey Chaucer, on whom he was an expert.

James DeCamp, her father, and Joseph Graydon, her mother's father, were both lawyers. They all lived in Cincinnati, a solid middle-western Republican city, which was the home of the Tafts, one of whom – William Howard Taft – had been President; the most recent Senator Robert Taft was accepted as an elder statesman of the Republicans. Brought up during Prohibition, Caroline's parents were quite heavy drinkers, and every night people came for drinks on the terrace while the meal was cooked, and then went on to drink late into the night.

My future mother-in-law, Anne DeCamp, had a social life of her own and was involved in the Widows and Old Folks Fêtes, which she helped organise to raise money. Her husband James was a golfer and enjoyed nothing more than a day on the links. I also became good friends with Caroline's sister Nance and brother Graydon.

They had all the normal prejudices of their generation, and no idea at all about equal rights for the African-Americans. When my son Hilary was asked by his great-grandfather on a family visit to Cincinnati what he especially noticed about America, Hilary replied, 'Well, the police have guns, and the Africans do all the work!' He was about six at the time and his great-grandfather laughed.

Cincinnati is an old river town on the Ohio and across the water lies Kentucky, which had been one of the Confederate states in the war, so that slaves would escape across the water into Ohio, before civil war ended slavery throughout the United States.

Following my introduction to Caroline's family, I began some months of travelling as a salesman for Benn Brothers' publications – and a miserably lonely and unsuccessful trip it was. With paper rationing, British magazines were slim compared to the bulky journals that were available in the States. I moved from city to city staying in little hotels, culling the names of potential customers from the Yellow Pages and going round with my wares, always to be treated kindly, but with practically nothing whatsoever to show for it.

Because Benn Brothers had some connections with McGraw Hill in New York, in the spring of 1949 I took a little room on the west of Manhattan and worked at their HQ, where I learned a lot about publishing and editing and got on well as a student of modern American marketing methods. Then, in the summer, I was free, returned to Caroline's home and we were married from there at the Church of the Advent, which was her local church. We went on to a honeymoon in Michigan in a cottage that her parents had rented, and from there to the Summer Institute for Social Progress at Wellesley College, where I spoke in the debate about the future of Europe and the world.

The story of the bureaucracy I encountered in order to marry Caroline is an amusing one. In Britain I had applied for a visitor's visa from the American Embassy to allow me to go over to get married. The embassy replied saying that, if I was going to marry an American girl, it would only grant me an immigration visa, since nobody going to America to marry would ever want to leave.

This posed a problem, because I was still on the reserve list as a Fleet Air Arm pilot and could be recalled at any time, so I had to ask the Admiralty if they would agree to release me; I received a letter from them granting me permission to emigrate, adding in a formal note that the Lords Commissioners of the Admiralty wished me all success in my future life!

When I arrived in America, the US authorities wrote to welcome me, offering to provide courses in English for all immigrants – an offer for which I thanked them, but said that I did not need.

After we were married we left for England, as we had planned, and on my return home I got another letter from the United States asking me if I had left America to avoid military service. Meanwhile, under British law at that time, Caroline had to be registered as an alien, and was required to report to the police, and whenever she went more than fifty miles from London the police also had to be notified. This, on one occasion, led to the police calling at our front door to see if she was there.

If she had applied for British citizenship, as she was entitled to do, she would have had to renounce her American citizenship and take an oath of allegiance to the Crown, which, on principle, she was not prepared to do, being very proud of her US citizenship. When I once told this story in a parliamentary debate on immigration law, a Tory MP attacked me bitterly for not having insisted that she become British, and said it was a disgrace that as an MP I had allowed her to retain her US citizenship.

Caroline and I returned to Britain after our honeymoon on a French liner, the *Île de France*. As she had not had time to put her married name on her passport, the French stewards tried to be very understanding and nodded and smiled at each other, as if to say it did not matter that we were not married – and perhaps they had underestimated the British in matters of love.

After two months at home with my folks, we moved into a flat in Goldhawk Road, Hammersmith, where the rent was £115 per year. I got a job at the BBC at £9 per week as a producer in the North American Service, where I was able to do everything, including editing, interviewing and introducing programmes on subjects that I mainly picked myself, and which were transmitted by shortwave and re-broadcast on public-service stations.

Among the people whom I asked to broadcast was Bernard Shaw; and I received from him one of his famous postcards, the address hand-written by him and with the following printed message:

Mr Bernard Shaw's readers and the spectators at performances of his plays number many thousands. The little time remaining to him at his age is fully occupied with his literary work and the business it involves; and war taxation has set narrow limits to his financial resources. He has therefore to print the following intimations.

He cannot deal with individual grievances and requests for money, nor for autographs and photographs. He cannot finance schools and churches. His donations go to undenominational public bodies and his charities go to the Royal Society of Literature.

He cannot engage in private correspondence, nor read long letters.

He cannot advise literary beginners nor read their unpublished works. They had better study the Writers' Year Book (or other books of reference), and join the Society of Authors as associates.

He cannot discuss his published views in private letters.

He cannot receive visits at his private residence except from his intimate friends.

<u>He will not send messages.</u>

He begs to be excused accordingly.

Ayot Saint Lawrence
Welwyn Herts
2/4/1950

Having campaigned in the Abbey Division of Westminster in the 1945 General Election (and distributed leaflets as a lad of ten in the 1935 election), I was approached by the Abbey party in 1946 – by then I was twenty-one – to seek my nomination to 'List B'. This was the list compiled by the party headquarters at Transport House with the names and details of party members whom constituency parties believed would be suitable for adoption as candidates by the Labour Party.

All it meant was that, if you were adopted by a constituency anywhere in the country to fight a seat, the local constituency party concerned would know something about you. When a vacancy for a candidate occurred, List B would be made available to the local party to give them some idea of people they might want to interview. The choice of candidate still had to be endorsed by the National Executive Committee, but there would be the safeguard that the person chosen was on List B. All that has now changed of course because the National Executive controls much more tightly the selection of candidates, particularly at by-elections.

One local party that approached me was Richmond, in June 1950, but I refused them for reasons that were explained in my letter to them:

> . . . I am in rather a difficult position at the moment, so I am afraid that my answer will have to be no. I work in the BBC, which, as you know, prohibits all political activity. If I were nominated I would have to give up my job at once. I have been to Transport House to talk over the problem with Mr Windle, especially to ask if I should have my name taken off the list. But he has advised me to keep it on anyway and to try and find another job . . .

> I would not be able to devote all my energies to the constituency, to say nothing of any other kind of backing. Besides, I have recently got married and that is an additional complication.

> Again thank you for your offer . . .

I had earlier been approached by John Parker, an MP who became Father of the House, during the war; he was on the lookout for young Labour candidates and asked me if I would put my name forward, but as I was then only nineteen I had to ask to be excused.

However, by the time Raymond Blackburn, Labour MP, left the Party in 1950 and his Northfield constituency in Birmingham was looking for a new candidate, I had decided that I would give up my BBC job, if successful. I agreed to attend the selection conference, but before it was held Bristol South East approached me because their MP Sir Stafford Cripps, the Chancellor of the Exchequer (who had cancer), was retiring.

The approach came from Mervyn Stockwood, the rector of St Matthew Moorfield in my constituency, who was also a Labour councillor and later became Bishop of Southwark. I believe that my friend Tony Crosland, by then the MP for South Gloucestershire, had suggested me to Stockwood, so on 1 November Caroline and I set out by car on my first ever visit to Bristol for my first ever selection conference, knowing no one and having no hope of winning. Arthur Creech Jones, the Colonial Secretary who was born in Bristol and whose brother was a Labour councillor there, had lost his seat of Shipley in the February 1950 election, and the by-election offered a natural opportunity to him to return to Parliament and Government. Another candidate had also been a Labour MP: Muriel Nichol, the daughter of Dick Wallhead (also a former Labour MP), who had lost her seat at the same time.

The national agent of the Labour Party had come down to be sure that Creech Jones was selected, and the regional organiser was also there for the same reason. What I did not know was that having had a Cabinet minister as their MP for five years, Bristol South East desperately wanted some young candidate who would work with the constituency and not be siphoned off into high office.

One serious shadow hung over my candidature in that my dad, who was then seventy-three, would, when he died, saddle me with his wretched peerage and I would be disqualified. I pointed this out, but they didn't seem to mind; and when I was asked what money I could give to the constituency if I was the candidate, I replied that this was not a Tory selection conference and if I did have money to give, I certainly wouldn't tell them at this stage. They also asked me if I would move to Bristol to live, if I was their MP. I said, 'I have just got married, we are hoping for a family and I really would want to be with them at the weekend, but promise that I will always be here whenever you want me.'

After all the candidates had finished their statements, we were brought in together to hear the result, which I thought was rather brutal. After I won, both Creech Jones and Mrs Nichol warmly congratulated me, which was typically generous of both of them.

Polling day was 30 November and that day President Truman said, almost casually, that he might use an atomic bomb in the Korean War. But on polling day no busy candidate has time to listen to the news, and it was only later that I heard this devastating threat, which led Attlee to fly to Washington immediately to deflect Truman.

So it was that on 4 December 1950, at the age of twenty-five, I took the oath and my seat, with my parents and my brother in the gallery. I was technically 'baby of the house' (that is, youngest member of the Commons) for twenty-four hours. The circumstances were interesting because another Member, Tom Teevan, who was two years younger than I, was elected in a by-election on 29 November 1950 in Belfast West, but did not take his seat until the day after me.

Thus, with the threat of a peerage overshadowing me, began a life in the Commons that ended in May 2001, more than fifty years later, with a few interruptions. I had served in Parliament longer than any other Labour MP in the history of the Party.

My campaign to rid myself of the peerage began in 1955, five years before my father died. I introduced a private bill in that year and appeared before the Private Bill Committee of the House of Lords, in the Moses Room, to present my case, backed up by a petition from the Lord Mayor, Aldermen and Burgesses of Bristol and by the Bishop of Bristol. That committee dismissed my claim.

My father then introduced a public bill in the Lords, which was also defeated. That is why when he died in 1960 at the age of eighty-three, I found myself excluded and was taken to the Privileges Committee of the House of Commons, which demanded that I produce my parents' marriage certificate, my elder brother's death certificate and my own birth certificate, as the basis on which it recommended my exclusion from the Commons.

Throughout this whole period my mother and father, and Caroline and my family, supported my campaign unhesitatingly. Indeed, Caroline was most passionate in her views.

A few months after my exclusion my seat was declared vacant and a by-election occurred to find a successor. At that time there was a loophole in the law, which enabled electoral officers (in my case the Town Clerk of Bristol) to accept as candidates all persons who were 'properly nominated' – even if disqualified for some reason, as I was. Thus I was actually able to stand as the Labour candidate despite the peerage complication. One minor consequence of my campaign was that this loophole was later closed.

I was duly re-elected with a much bigger majority, having circulated to my constituents a letter of support from Winston Churchill and having received backing from a range of people. I therefore turned up at the House of Commons as the newly elected Member of Parliament and the Speaker told the Doorkeeper, Victor Stockley, that if I tried to enter the Chamber to take my seat, he was to keep me out – 'if necessary by force'.

My Tory opponent, Malcolm St Clair (who, unbelievably, was also the heir to a peerage), took me to an election court presided over by two judges sitting alone, and I presented my own case after spending months studying peerage law with the help of Michael Zander; I found myself up against two QCs.

My initial speech took about four days to deliver. At the end the judges reported that I was disqualified on the basis of a judgement by Mr Justice Dodderidge, who in 1626 ruled that a peerage was 'an incorporeal hereditament affixed in the blood and annexed to the posterity', which (loosely interpreted) meant that it was a bit of real property in my blood that I could not get rid of.

On that basis, the candidate I had beaten was seated in the House as the new MP for Bristol South East and I was out in the wilderness, with no prospect of serving in the Commons again.

However, public support for my campaign, reflected also in the by-election result, led the Tory government to set up a select committee to look at the matter. In the summer of 1963 it recommended that an heir to a peerage could renounce within six months of succession. But when the Peerage Bill that included this provision went to the Commons, they made an amendment to exclude peerages that had *already* been inherited. This would have kept me out for ever.

Strangely, it was the House of Lords which reversed that amendment and allowed me to benefit. It may possibly be that one reason was that the Earl of Home was a potential candidate for the leadership of the Tory Party when Macmillan resigned (which he did later that year, on health grounds), and so they wanted to keep the door open for him. At any rate the bill was passed and I was sitting in the gallery of the House of Lords when the Royal Assent was given. When the words '*La Reine le veult*' were spoken, I shot out of the gallery and the door banged audibly, then I went to the Lord Chancellor's office with my Instrument of Renunciation and became a free man.

One amusing aspect of this was that when I went into the Lord Chancellor's office, the Doorkeeper said, 'Good afternoon, my Lord' and as I left he said, 'Goodbye, sir'.

Malcolm St Clair then resigned from the Commons, there was a further by-election, and I was returned again as the MP for Bristol South East in the autumn of 1963.

What I learned from it all was that an appeal for justice taken to the top rarely succeeds and it was the backing of my constituents and of the Constituency Labour Party that forced the government to shift – a strange way, you may think, to learn what every socialist has always known: that all progress comes from below, and that struggle has to be waged there.

Just before I renounced my peerage, I went to hospital and a kind doctor took some blue blood out of me, which I wanted to keep, since I knew I was about to lose it. I still have it in a bottle, and though the blood is clotted now, it would have been a ticket to a seat in Parliament (the Lords) for life, if I had been ready to accept the peerage.

When I left the Commons in 2001, Mr Speaker Martin recognised the fact that Ted Heath and I had both served for fifty years and conferred upon us both the new honour of 'Freedom of the House', which entitles us to use the Tea Room, the Library and the Cafeteria, and even to sit in the peers' gallery of the House of Commons if we want to attend debates there. I therefore enjoy all the privileges of peerage without the humiliation of actually being a lord!

Throughout my political life, until her death in November 2000 (just before I retired), Caroline had been my sternest and most rigorous critic. Unlike me, she was a real intellectual, with a mind that could get to the bottom of any issue. Whenever I would submit a text to her for advice, she would read it and ask, 'Well, what are you really trying to say?' which sent me off to start afresh.

During our early years she had the four children to look after: Stephen, our eldest who has worked for many years as the Parliamentary officer of the Royal Society of Chemistry; Hilary, now an MP and in the Cabinet; Melissa, a writer, novelist and broadcaster; and Joshua, who is responsible for IT work in the Housing Corporation. The friendships she formed with them were deep and real, thinking about their needs and characters, just as she did later about our ten grandchildren, giving her full attention to them – a quality she showed to all her many friends around the world. She kept up a formidable correspondence with them almost to the day of her death.

Marriage to a Member of Parliament is a very demanding assignment and, despite her later reservations about the parliamentary world, Caroline would come willingly to the constituency and to meetings, and accepted the disruption to normal family life that Parliament involved and which made me a very inconsiderate partner.

She loved music and enjoyed going to concerts with her many friends, not least to Wexford with Peter Carter and to the Cincinnati Music Festival, which she attended whenever she could, travelling alone and combining it with a tour of her American relatives.

Her interest in education began in earnest when, having sent our children to Holland Park Comprehensive School, she became a governor there and served as Chair for twelve of her twenty-four years with the school, later being co-opted onto the LEA in London, which appointed her to be a governor of Imperial College and Mary Datchelor Girls' School. Later she began to teach for the Open University, being a passionate believer in adult education. This continued when she taught at our local college, only retiring at seventy.

She became a keen gardener in London and at Stansgate, where she bought a field and turned it into a nature reserve. Her concerns about the environment were real and led her to campaign actively on environmental issues. Both of us became vegetarians, converted by our son, Hilary, on the grounds both of agricultural economy and animal welfare.

But the real contribution Caroline made was as a writer about, and campaigner for, comprehensive education, working with Professor Brian Simon to produce a book entitled *Halfway There* which recorded the progress made by every local education authority.

Later, with Professor Clyde Chitty, she wrote a second book called *Thirty Years On*, which carried the story forward. And as a founder of the Campaign for Comprehensive Education, she moved on to be President of the Socialist Education Association and wrote many articles for learned journals about every aspect of education. She also headed up a Labour movement study of the work of the Manpower Services Commission, attending endless meetings and seminars, but never seeking any publicity for herself.

Her speaking style was quite unique: having prepared every word with the care that would normally be given to a university lecture, she stood rigidly, without a gesture, and spoke so softly that it was hard to hear it; but she was always listened to in absolute silence with rapt attention.

Apart from her novel, *Lion in a Den of Daniels*, which was published in England and America, her one major book was a life of Keir Hardie, which was recognised as the best account of the formation of the Labour Party. Caroline travelled to Scotland,

America and the Netherlands to collect material for it, and received wonderful reviews from Tony Blair and Gordon Brown.

Her formidable archives (unfortunately not as well indexed as they should be) will be a source of immense interest to generations of scholars, and I hope they will find a home where they can be widely studied.

Caroline was very tough, and the guiding commitment in her life and work was to equality, democracy and socialism; she gave me the Communist Manifesto for Christmas one year, knowing that I had not read it and that I should understand the meaning of Marxism if I was to be any good in politics.

Two annual lectures in her memory take place every year, and a book of essays on education and democracy, dedicated to her, has been published.

But there was a great deal more to her than that, for she was a woman of strong character and immense courage, revealed when in her last four years she suffered from a serious cancer and decided that she would not fight it, but would live with it to enjoy every remaining moment that she had.

She taught me how to live and how to die, and you cannot ask any more of anyone than that: loving, caring, thoughtful, critical when necessary, always understanding and forgiving. I had the good fortune and the privilege of living with her, and learning from her, for so long and she was the centrepiece of my life and of the life of my family.

We discussed my decision not to stand again for Chesterfield and it was she who suggested that I should explain it by saying that 'I was giving up Parliament to spend more time on politics'.

Part Three

Now: Essays and

Speeches

Benn

PLAIN SPEAKING and HARD WORK FOR HIS CONSTITUENTS PLACES THE LABOUR MANIFESTO

TONY BENN firmly BELIEVES in the need for:-

- Full employment.
- A big house building programme.
- A free health service and better care for the disabled.
- Life long and equal education for everyone.
- Higher pensions and dignity for all retired men and women.
- A minimum wage, better benefits and a fairer tax system.
- Democratic reform, civil liberties and trade union rights.
- Freedom for local authorities to provide essential services.
- An end to all forms of discrimination.
- World peace, disarmament and development.
- The protection of the planet and its wild-life from destruction.

HE SOLEMNLY PLEDGES that he will CONSCIENTIOUSLY WORK

for THESE OBJECTIVES

Labour

Introduction

The themes explored in Part Three reflect both the lasting influence of my parents, and their interests and concerns, and my own experiences during more than half a century of war, peace and political activity. The first four essays set out a reassessment of the role of a Member of Parliament, of the reality of ministerial office in government, and of the prospects of peace and of a new British foreign and defence policy in a challenging and dangerous world dominated by an American empire. These essays are followed by speeches, made in my last years as a Member of Parliament, which restate my enduring interest in and commitment to peace, justice, democracy and socialism.

I have described how my father and my grandfathers had all served as MPs and how I hoped that I too would follow in their footsteps. My growing up was therefore dominated by the idea of public service. I began my parliamentary life seeing the pursuit of social justice and peace as achievable through the Labour movement in Parliament. I then believed that the situation was getting better, although more slowly than I had hoped. Now it sometimes seems that the situation is getting worse, more rapidly than I feared.

If the skill and money now available were spent on resolving the world's problems, instead of preparing for Armageddon against communists, terrorists or whoever else dares to challenge the hegemony of the wealthy, there is nothing we could not achieve if we turned our minds to it. The relationship between social justice, peace, democracy and internationalism now dominates my thinking.

I have lived to see the defeat of the Nazis, the ratification of the Charter of the United Nations, the establishment of the welfare state and the development of a National Health Service (all of which are now under threat), and a welcome end to the old European empires. There has been some progress in women's rights, with equal pay legislation and more recently the ordination of women in the Church of England – a cause for which my mother campaigned for much of her life.

Like my father, I have found myself moving politically to the left as I have got older. The reason in both cases is similar: experience taught us that democracy does not just mean electing someone to government every five years, but achieving progress through collective effort and a clear understanding of where power truly rests.

In medieval times power was exercised by kings, conquerors and land owners, and in more recent times by multinational corporations, the military and the media. Effective democracy has to develop beyond the idea of an elected Parliament to the exercise of greater control over all these powers that determine our destiny.

Democracy is what we do for ourselves wherever we live and

work. History is rich with examples of exactly that, whether we are talking about trade unionism, the campaign for votes for men and later for women, the end of apartheid, the colonial liberation movements or the actions of environmental campaigners. Democracy is always a struggle for justice against the powerful.

For that reason I have come increasingly to realise that for any such advances to be made, people have to argue publicly and be ready to organise to win support and carry through change, when there is a popular majority for it: that is why I believe the Labour Party, organically linked to the trade unions and with socialists in it, here and worldwide, is so important.

As any member of the Labour Party will attest, there are many disappointments and moments of despair (if not anger) at decisions taken by successive Labour governments. But it remains true that without such a collective instrument as the Labour Party, little progress is possible; and those who advocate progressive policies have first to win the argument within the Party, if they are ever to win a popular majority.

But if the Labour Party is to rediscover its historical mission, it has to reconnect the working-class movement with the radical tradition and develop as a much more internationalist party, concerned with peace, justice, democracy and human rights – themes that I explore in the following pages.

The emergence of New Labour as a neo-Thatcherite party deeply committed to capitalism, and acting as a junior partner in a new imperial mission launched in Washington, has gravely damaged the appeal of the Party to those who put their hopes in it. However, I am hopeful that this phase is ending, and my hopes are shared by many millions of others who sense that we need a new direction for this century.

1

The Reality of Parliament

Being an MP is unique. It is the only job where there is one employee and 60,000 employers, for everyone in your constituency has the right to remove you. And that is what forces MPs to listen – a burden not carried by peers who have their seats for life.

The correspondence of an MP is massive, and the surgeries or advice centres long and tiring. But it is the pastoral side of being an MP that is most rewarding, though it hardly ever merits any public description or discussion.

Certainly most of what I learned derived from my constituency and the people in it, and it was no good trying to thrust ideology down constituents' throats when they needed a pension or house or job; you had to tackle the problem as *they* saw it, and then think out what policy change was necessary to prevent similar problems from recurring in the future.

The constituency work of an MP began when Lloyd George introduced National Insurance, and I remember my father telling me that a Tory MP came into the Members' Post Office at the

Commons, was handed four letters that had arrived for him and threw them down, complaining, 'That is what your Mr Lloyd George has done for us!', resenting the workload he had to take on.

Father also said that before women got the vote, important social questions were discussed in a way that resembled a gentleman's club more than a modern House of Commons.

Ever since I was a child I always had the aspiration of serving as a Labour MP. My dad was always described as a 'good parliamentarian', a man who loved the place and was respected there, and that description has sometimes been applied to me too. I always regarded it as an honour to be so described. But when I look back on my life, I am beginning to see the work of a modern Parliament in a rather different light.

Father always told me as a child that the key to parliamentary government was that the House of Commons *controlled the purse and the sword*, and that *no Parliament can bind its successor*. This was a clear and bold claim to make, but one that has been completely transformed in all respects in the last half-century or more.

The modern House of Commons does not now *control the purse*, because the interaction of the world economy and the institutions that it has created, in banking and the development of multinational corporations, has locked England so tightly into that system that it is not in the power of any government – even the American government – to escape from the pressures and decisions imposed on it by those who are in no sense democratically elected or accountable. Of course absolute economic freedom has never been possible, even when the economy was in its early stages, in that investment had to be arranged and markets had to be found.

But when I look back at my own opportunities to study this system in greater detail, very vivid examples come to mind of the extent of our subservience to the new world economic order, sometimes described as globalisation.

But free trade, that old Liberal principle on which my father had been brought up, was a very good example of the regulation of commerce to prevent it from distortions created by national governments, which might create tensions that could lead to trade wars, and thence real wars.

On the other hand, free trade, as now imposed by GATT or the WTO or the IMF, denies elected governments the right to take action to protect those they represent, and we have had very real experience of that over my years in Parliament.

The balance of payments dominated the politics of the Wilson and Callaghan governments and led them to make cuts that damaged Labour's prospects of re-election, although nowadays we are told that the balance of payments doesn't matter.

The cuts imposed on the Callaghan government in 1976 by the IMF were accompanied with a blunt warning that, if it did not comply with these demands, the British economy would be ruined. So the Cabinet capitulated after long and anxious discussions in which I put forward an alternative economic strategy, which was nevertheless rejected.

I was told that my proposals involved a siege economy, and I argued that the IMF was imposing a siege economy (except that in their siege the bankers would be inside the castle with a Labour government, and the castle would be besieged by our supporters) – a prediction that turned out to be right because the cuts triggered the so-called Winter of Discontent in 1979 and made possible the election of Margaret Thatcher. That government mounted a massive counter-revolution against trade unions, local government, the welfare state and democracy itself. That counter-revolution was confirmed and entrenched when New Labour came to power, on the grounds that we had no alternative, as Thatcher used to say, but to live in the real world, which requires us to carry on many of the policies she initiated.

More recently we have seen the impact of the European Community membership on our freedom of action. Under the provisions of the Maastricht Treaty and the stability pact, the Central Bank in Frankfurt (which is not elected) working with the Commission (which is not elected) has laid down that no government in the new European Union can borrow or spend more than 3 per cent of its national income, a policy that forces governments to privatise if they wish to expand their public services without infringing the new rules.

This policy has recently been tested because the French and Germans, facing serious economic problems, have breached those rules and the Commission is now engaged in trying to enforce them (through the European Court). This could, if it succeeded, lead to the defeat of governments that stood against the iron law of Maastricht.

In the light of this and many other examples, it can no longer be truthfully said that the House of Commons controls the purse; and ministers are little more than branch bank managers carrying out the policy of the main board, which exercises its sway over the globe.

This is also true of our *control of the sword*. The phrase derives from the Glorious Revolution of 1688 when the power of the King to raise and maintain armed forces against the wishes of Parliament, which had been the source of royal power for centuries, was limited and was controlled by the Army Annual Act. The act required the House of Commons to re-enact every year the power to have forces, and if there was some theoretical conflict with the

King, he would be denied the right to command and pay such forces, which would lose their legal authority.

Looking back on it, that was a considerable victory at the time and, as a young Member, I attended and sometimes spoke in the debate on the Army Annual Act and was proud that we had retained that power – and in theory could use it again, if it was ever necessary.

But of course in recent years that has changed completely. I suppose this change can be attributed to the Second World War, when American forces were based in Britain and played a leading role in mounting the assault on D-Day that gave the Allies victory over the Axis powers, and when the American forces remained in Britain permanently after the war.

The dominant political forces were no longer British, but American under the command of an American President, whom we did not elect and could not remove. The command of NATO was in the hands of an American general, from Eisenhower through to the present day.

The true position is that we no longer control the sword in any meaningful sense, and Britain's nuclear weapons' programme has always been kept a tight secret from which MPs are excluded.

Today, when questions are asked about the location of nuclear weapons (even British ones) in any part of the world, the standard government answer is that they will neither confirm nor deny. So we are in a permanent state of ignorance imposed on us by the executive.

This situation becomes even more complex when you realise, as I came to do when I was Minister of Technology responsible for the civil nuclear programme, that Britain does not have an independent nuclear deterrent any more, since the cancellation of the Vulcan bomber (which was capable of dropping primitive nuclear bombs) and the adoption of first Polaris and then Trident missiles. The technology for these weapons was so complex that it was beyond the industrial and scientific capacity of Britain to develop them. They are made available to us by the US, which also controls the global satellite guidance system without which, even if they were fired by a British Prime Minister, they could not be guided to their target and would rise and fall ineffectively.

In truth, Britain does not have an independent deterrent, although we count ourselves as a nuclear power, which we are not – unlike the French, whose Force de Frappe does give the President of France some limited scope for independent action.

In return for assisting Britain in this pretence, the American government has laid down very strict rules that allow it to control our intelligence services and (as at GCHQ) to have access to all the intelligence we have, including material gathered by bugging communications in Britain – a process that National Missile Defence (the so-called 'Star Wars' system) will consolidate and extend.

So tight is this control that when the government decided to proceed with the enrichment of uranium using the centrifuge, I had to go, as a minister, and get permission from a special hearing at the Atomic Energy Commission in Washington, chaired by Glenn Seaborg. And until that permission was granted, Britain would not have been able to proceed.

The nature of this subservience in nuclear matters must have been one of the dominant factors persuading Tony Blair to go along, uncritically, with President Bush's decision to invade Iraq in 2003. For he must have known that if he had stood by our commitment to the UN Charter and opposed that war, Britain would have run the risk of losing its pretence to be a nuclear power and would be revealed as a non-nuclear island off the coast of Europe, of interest to Washington only because its bombers could fly from British bases.

The role and importance of civil nuclear power have to be understood because when the bombs were dropped at Hiroshima and Nagasaki, the human race had a warning that it dared not ignore. But ten years later, when Eisenhower announced his policy of Atoms for Peace and launched the civil nuclear-power programme, many people became really excited at the thought that 'we were turning swords into ploughshares', and I advocated civil nuclear power with real passion and commitment.

It was only when I had responsibility for nuclear power that I realised that it was not cheap, safe or peaceful. That discovery turned me into a passionate opponent of civil nuclear power because it was dangerous, expensive and from the beginning was all about the development of plutonium for military purposes.

After I had left office, I discovered that while I had been there supporting nuclear power for civil purposes, the plutonium we generated in our power stations was actually going into the American nuclear weapons programme and every one of our stations was in truth an atom-bomb factory.

The principle that *no Parliament can bind its successor* is also no longer valid, thus defying Tom Paine's famous statement that 'the dead cannot control the living'. For nowadays, through NATO and our membership of the EU and in many other ways, one Parliament can and does commit its successors. And more and more people are coming to realise that whoever they vote for in future elections, they cannot alter the policies adopted by the government that has just been defeated.

This realisation is already widening the gap between the people and the Parliament they elect; it could explain the falling turnout at elections, which in itself could undermine the democratic legitimacy of future governments and encourage people to believe that direct action – and even riot – may turn out to be the best way of securing political objectives.

If that view were to prevail, it would entail the death of parliamentary democracy and the consequences would be very serious – not only for the people, who would lose their representation, but also for those with power, because we should not forget that democracy was demanded by those who wanted their rights, but was conceded because it was safer for those in authority to retain their power by consent than by force.

I think that the English revolution so frightened the British establishment that, unlike the French establishment, which risked a revolution and the guillotine that followed rather than make any concessions, the powers-that-be here would see that conceding certain limited powers could defuse the opposition before they took to the streets.

Shocking though it is to say so, I have concluded that one of the reasons why the powerful continue to boast of parliamentary democracy is because they see it as the most effective means of defusing their critics. One way is to claim that we are a perfect democracy and that the people can remove governments they do not like and elect ones they do like, and that is what democracy is about. But for the reasons I have set out above, that is not strictly true, although the capacity to get rid of a government without killing anyone is an important power that many people around the world would give their life to possess in their own country.

So when pressure for change builds up to the point where it cannot be resisted, the British establishment has developed a way of dealing with it, by withdrawing in an apparent desire to concede some of the claims and then decapitating some of the radical movements by appearing to give them power. For example, by promoting the leaders of these movements and putting them in the House of Lords, some militant trade unionists of earlier years (some of them ex-communists) sit on the red benches and feel they have been rewarded for their work, when actually they have been politically castrated by their ennoblement.

The limitations on the power of MPs are also very severe, arising mainly from the crude use of patronage by the leader of their own party and by the exercise of the royal prerogative by the Prime Minister of the day, which of course goes far beyond patronage.

A young MP who wants to be promoted must not displease his party leader, and a member of the government faces dismissal if he angers the Prime Minister who appointed him. Older members hoping for retirement in the House of Lords also know that it is the Prime Minister who commands the honours lists and who can grant or withhold their wish.

Within the party, the leader nowadays has immense powers that can lead to the expulsion of MPs, or he can exercise his influence to make reselection as a candidate more difficult, if not impossible. Then there is the crude use of loyalty by a party leader to secure policies he wishes to carry out through a blanket threat – that 'defiance' of the leader could lead to overall defeat for the party in an election.

In saying this I am not opposed to the party system, because I believe that individuals cannot make much progress without the strength of the collective. But MPs could do far more to assert the authority which their own constituents have given them over the executive; they have been far too compliant in bowing to the wishes of the Whips and the orders of Downing Street, as with the recent three-line whip, first to oppose a referendum on the European Union's proposed constitution and then to support it.

If the House of Commons were to decide (as it could) to exercise far greater control over the executive – as, for example, in making the exercise of the royal prerogative subject to the approval of the Commons – Parliament could work much more effectively and public confidence in it could be restored in part.

Also Members of Parliament should speak more boldly and clearly, and should not fear that a word out of place could endanger their position, so long as the speeches made are not personal or offensive in character.

I have always divided MPs into two categories – signposts and weathercocks – and I admire signposts more than weathercocks, the latter having no opinion until the polls have been scrutinised and the focus groups interrogated to show the way forward.

What is required is a much more radical approach to the meaning of democracy, which must be about people's own conception of their role and their determination to force any government to listen. When the pressure is off, the system reverts, as it is now doing, to a medieval monarchy in which the King governs and Parliament merely advises.

Looking back therefore, after many years in Parliament and with many friends in the House of Commons, I am confirmed in my belief that it is an instrument capable of making important changes for the betterment of the community. But the pressure to do so must begin at the bottom, be advanced by those who sit in the Commons and implemented by governments that see themselves as servants, and not as masters.

2

Whitehall Behind Closed Doors

It is widely believed by many members of the public that all politicians, and especially ministers, are untrustworthy and self-seeking. And it is assumed by some on the left that all Labour governments have betrayed their commitment to socialism, as if every Labour MP begins life as a dedicated socialist and gives up ideology when he or she gets to Parliament or becomes a minister.

This is not my experience of my colleagues at all, and cynicism is utterly destructive of the democratic process – unlike argument, which sustains democracy.

Therefore to make sense of what is going on we have at least to see ministerial office in its true light, since being a minister is one of the most interesting, difficult, challenging and exhausting jobs that an MP can have. Most MPs would like ministerial office. Without the experience, it is extremely difficult for anyone to understand how governments work, the limitations under which they have to operate, the choices they have to make and the responsibility that rests upon their shoulders.

I was lucky to get my first appointment as head of the Post Office – the now abolished position of Postmaster-General – when I was thirty-nine years old. I found myself thrown into the headquarters of the Post Office at St Martin's le Grand, which employed a huge number of people, including all the postmen, counter clerks, telephone operators and engineers at what was the centre of Britain's communications system. And this job was combined with that of being the sponsoring minister for the broadcasting organisations.

Harold Wilson had dropped a hint when we were at the Durham Miners' Gala in the summer of 1964 that he might appoint me, so I had a bit of time to prepare my thoughts. I had written an article about the future of the Post Office, suggesting that it was a model for the way a public service might develop and expand.

On assuming a government job for the first time after a General Election, every minister is handed a thick brief composed by his department, prepared in two drafts. The minister is given the appropriate one, depending on whether Labour or Conservatives have won the election. These briefs, written by officials who have read the party manifestos, tell you what the department would like you to do. I always kept them because they throw light on the subsequent minutes submitted to me with recommendations for future action.

My dad had always warned me to be careful, if ever I became a minister, because the officials would be very friendly. He particularly had in mind some MPs who within five minutes of becoming ministers were calling the Permanent Secretary by his Christian name and letting him get on with his job exactly as before.

In essence, the Civil Service offers an incoming minister a deal that sounds like this: 'Minister, if you do what we want you to do, we will help you to pretend you are doing what you said you would do.' And those who accept this deal have given up their basic right to take control of the department they purport to lead.

Certainly that was exactly how the Post Office was run in 1964; it was not a department at all, but a self-governing organism over which the Postmaster-General presided, receiving and automatically approving minutes from the Director-General of the Post Office – the equivalent of the Permanent Secretary.

I remember my private secretary, on coming to collect me from home for the first time in a giant Austin Princess limousine, asking me, 'How would you like to play it, PMG?' I very soon learned that my predecessor Reginald Bevins had turned up on Tuesdays and Thursdays at his office, where a long oblong table was covered in minutes from officials, which he would read and sign as he moved round the table, before going off to the House of Commons. My private office expected me to continue in that tradition and never to be there during parliamentary recesses. The Postmaster-General was seen as a sinecure position.

I naturally read the history of the Post Office from its earliest days and discovered from the memoirs of my predecessors, including Clem Attlee (who had held the job from 1929 to 1931), that they all felt it was absurd that the Post Office should be tied to the Treasury, paying all its receipts to it and receiving in return such money as was necessary to run the service. I suppose it would have been possible for me to continue on that care-and-maintenance basis and hope for promotion. I chose another path.

As any minister soon discovers, his most immediate allies are in the private office, whose job it is to help him deal with this vast permanent establishment which views each minister in much the same way as the staff of a luxury hotel would view an incoming distinguished visitor booked into the royal suite for an extended holiday. I had other ideas and began a series of intensive meetings to discuss the future of the Post Office, including a decision to convene the Post Office Board – which, like the Board of Trade, had not met for years but over which, in theory, I presided.

At these meetings I raised the issues I wanted to discuss and began issuing a series of numbered minutes of my own, making suggestions and asking questions. This was unusual, in that paperwork in the Civil Service starts at the bottom and is signed at the top; it doesn't normally start at the top. That must have been unsettling for the officials. I also appointed as my PPS a Labour MP called Charles Morris, who had himself worked in the Post Office and was a member of the Union of Post Office Workers. I was warned by the Director-General that, because of his trade-union background, this would be an inadvisable appointment.

I went and visited the UPW headquarters, which had never been done by a PMG before. And, guided by what Stafford Cripps had done as President of the Board of Trade after the war, I decided that wherever I went, I would hold a mass meeting for the staff to explain what I was trying to do, and would invite them to comment. This simple method, which included a huge gathering in the Royal Albert Hall concerning the future location of the Post Office Savings Bank, destabilised the mandarins, who felt they were ceding to the minister control that previously they had exercised themselves.

It was an immensely rewarding experience and I came to love the Post Office and its traditions, which represented the finest in Britain and which of course had been developed by Rowland Hill in the nineteenth century. The invention of the penny post had the same impact then as the Internet has had today, in that it allowed people to communicate with each other cheaply and introduced a cheaper printed paper rate, which allowed newspapers to go by mail.

I set all this out because the first experience of office, followed by appointment to the Cabinet two years later, gave me an understanding of the way that Labour ministers could shape policy, which could not have been learned any other way. Also, I learned the enormous value of having genuinely collective decision-making in the Cabinet itself, where key questions were discussed at length and decided sometimes by a vote; on one occasion a vote went against the manifest wishes of the Prime Minister. The Cabinet then comprised people of immense ability, including Wilson, Callaghan, Jenkins, Crosland, Castle, Crossman, Gardiner, and other giants of the period.

As far as I can make out, that tradition of discussion has been abandoned now in favour of much shorter meetings, in which the Prime Minister tells the Cabinet what he has decided and there is no real collective feel about it any more. Cabinet papers are no longer submitted by ministers to focus attention on issues that might not otherwise have reached Cabinet level.

Clearly, the question sometimes arises, 'Should a minister resign?' if his view in Cabinet is rejected. That question was often in my mind, and on one occasion I asked the Bristol South East Labour Party whether it would be right for me to resign, and I undertook to be guided by their decision. After a long debate they decided that they wished me to remain in Cabinet, but to argue my case as strongly as I could, which I think was right.

The consequences of a resignation have to be thought out. If a minister who resigns finds, as a backbencher, that he is required to vote on a motion of confidence in the House of Commons, does he then vote for the government he has just left? And if that government is defeated in Parliament and there is a General

Election, should he stand again as a parliamentary candidate to secure the re-election of the government whose policy he has specifically rejected by resignation? These are real questions and I concluded that it was right to stay and argue my case, winning some arguments and losing others – and then explaining in public what the decision that had been reached was, and why, even though I had taken a contrary view.

In the end, crude though it may be, those who vote and those who serve as ministers have to decide whether they still believe that the party to which they belong remains the lesser of two evils.

The freedom of action of a minister is not limited to the prejudices of a Prime Minister or the traditions of the department, but is imposed by a whole series of powers that lie quite outside parliamentary control: by treaty, by the imposition of international rules of finance, by the exercise of powerful influence by other countries (mainly the United States of America).

These cannot easily be brushed aside, but unfortunately ministers are reluctant to admit it, because they do not want to be thought of as not in charge, and they fear that if the truth were told, they would be revealed as puppets in the hands of others – which in a sense they are.

Unofficial restrictions include the ability to criticise mistakes made by the security services, so long as the power of those services is never challenged.

It is all right to criticise mistakes made by the Common Market or EU, but to question British membership is not permitted.

It is all right to comment on some absurd behaviour by a member of the royal family, but the legitimacy of the monarchy cannot be questioned.

It is all right to attack the excesses of the press, so long as the right of the proprietors to control the press is never brought into question.

I personally suffered because I was not prepared to accept these limitations.

Of course the satisfaction of ministerial office is enormous, because ministers do have powers to deal with problems that no backbencher has; and I can think of nothing more rewarding than to take decisions that really help people, particularly if the decision involves a battle with colleagues to get that decision agreed.

The limitations of collective Cabinet responsibility make it much harder to speak out, but I devised various techniques for bypassing it, which were just about within the rules although they were not popular with Number 10. For example, it was permissible to make a speech saying that in the years ahead – well beyond the life of the present Cabinet – the government would have to think of this and that, a method that put items on the agenda of public discussion, which would have been impossible if such proposals were made for immediate action.

Today, if even the most modest policy changes were made that involved any conflict with the IMF, the Central Bank in Frankfurt or the European Commission, or which angered the American President, Britain would be classified almost as a rogue state, with very serious consequences for those who had elected the government. This situation is not easily understood by electors and backbenchers who have never held office. It is one of the greatest single challenges to progressive governments in the future.

If there are criticisms to be made of Labour governments, it is not that they have betrayed the ideals of socialism, but that they have so often failed to fight for the people who elected them and to take action that would safeguard their interests.

3

The New Roman Empire

From the time when Julius Caesar landed in 55 BC and brought us into a single currency with the penny, up to the signing of the Treaty of Rome, Britain's relations with Europe have been central to the political debate in this country and still divide both parties in a way that has threatened their unity.

The immediate issue is the euro and whether Britain should join the European single currency; a secondary, but more important, question is whether we should accept a new European constitution drawn up under the chairmanship of the veteran French politician Giscard d'Estaing. The constitutional implications of European enlargement – which has brought in many Eastern European countries and produces a union of twenty-five, four times the size of the original six – are huge. A third question relates to whether or not Europe should have a common defence and foreign policy, in order, it is argued, that Europe is more united and can act as a counterweight to the United States.

At the outset of the Common Market I opposed it as a rich

men's club; subsequently, as a minister, I concluded that it was probably the only way of providing political supervision and control of multinational companies that were bigger than nation states; and I have now moved to the position where I see the EU's present form as representing a threat to democracy in Britain and throughout all the member states of the Union.

Harold Wilson changed his view on the matter, having first been against and then coming out in favour; and so did Mrs Thatcher, who was passionately in favour of Britain's membership in 1975 and signed the treaty that introduced the single market, but later, when out of office, opposed the Maastricht Treaty, the euro and all forms of European integration.

By contrast, Roy Jenkins, Michael Heseltine and Jo Grimond were united in support, as was Ted Heath, who signed the Treaty of Accession in 1972 without the authority of a referendum.

Talking to Ted Heath about this over the years, I have always found his arguments both simple and plainly political, for I have heard him say, 'Europe has had two major wars costing millions of lives and now we have got to get together.' And his fierce opposition to the Afghan, Iraq and Yugoslav wars confirmed my view that his position on Europe was based partly on his resentment of America dominating our continent.

That is an argument that has to be taken seriously, but since it raises constitutional questions, it would be intolerable if any steps taken to achieve it were slipped through Parliament without referenda to confirm them. Because these are all huge constitutional matters that involve taking away powers from the electors and transferring them into the hands of those who have been appointed.

Over the centuries Europe has seen many empires come and

go: Greek, Roman, Ottoman, French and German, not to mention Spanish, Portuguese and British. Many of the conflicts between European states have arisen from colonial rivalry between imperial powers.

The concert of Europe after the fall of Napoleon, in which countries would negotiate alternatives to war, gave way after 1919 to the League of Nations, dominated by the old imperial powers, and broke down in part because Mussolini's Italy launched a colonial war against Abyssinia in breach of the Charter of the League.

After the Second World War, western establishments had to consider how best to cooperate in rebuilding the continent and, as the Cold War began almost immediately, one of their objectives through NATO was to provide armed forces to prevent the Soviet Union from launching a military attack. It could therefore be argued that the EEC was set up to rebuild Europe on safe capitalist lines, and that NATO was set up to arm the EEC against the military threat that we were told was materialising.

Indeed, a few years ago I heard the former American Ambassador in London speaking at a reception in Speaker's House about the Marshall Plan, which, he openly declared, was an investment to prevent the spread of communism.

As Minister of Technology in 1969, facing the massive multinational corporations and wondering how a nation state could cope with them, I did begin to wonder whether the existence of the EEC might offer some opportunity for political control and ought to be considered for that reason. Such a huge step required popular consent, and that was why in 1970 when we were in opposition and I was free to speak, I argued the case for a referendum to seek the consent of the British people. I discovered that the idea of a referendum was absolutely unacceptable to the establishment, which was totally opposed to giving the people direct say in any decisions, least of all one that might frustrate their dream of a Europe controlled by the political elite.

The referendum itself, held in 1975 after Heath had lost the 1974 election, was fought in a way that revealed the imbalance of money and influence on the two sides – the pro-Europe campaign having the support of the establishment and every single newspaper except the *Morning Star*, and able to command enormous resources; while the anti-campaign even had to struggle to find the cash to hold press conferences and meetings.

Wilson moved me from Industry to Energy immediately afterwards and I found myself on the council of energy ministers, where I served until 1970 and had the opportunity of seeing how the Common Market mechanism worked.

During the British presidency in 1977 I was the President of the Council of Energy Ministers. It is the only committee I have ever sat on in my life where as a member, or even as President, I was not allowed to submit a document – a right confined to the unelected Commission, leaving ministers like some collective monarch in a constitutional monarchy, able only to say Yes or No.

The Council of Ministers is of course the real parliament, for the directives and decisions take effect in member states without endorsement by the national parliaments. Because it is in effect a parliament, I proposed during my presidency that it should meet in public, so that everyone could see how decisions are reached and what arguments are used. This sent a chill of horror through the other ministers, who feared that it would bring to light the little deals that were used to settle differences, and I lost.

I also came to realise that the EEC – far from being an instrument for the political control of multinationals – was actually welcomed by the multinationals, which saw it as a way of overcoming the policies of national governments to which they objected.

For example, I was advised by the Energy Commissioner that the North Sea oil really belonged to Europe and was told by my own officials that the 1946 Atomic Energy Act in Britain, which gave the then government control of all atomic operations, had been superseded by Euratom (the European Atomic Energy Community) and that we no longer had any power of control.

I was warned that national support for industrial companies was a breach of the principle of free trade and was threatened with action if I disregarded their rules.

It became clear over the succeeding thirty years that the European Union, as it became, is a carefully constructed mechanism for eliminating all democratic influences hitherto exercised by the electors in the member states; it presents this as a triumph of internationalism, when it is a reversal of democratic gains made in the previous hundred years.

Now, with the Maastricht Treaty, the Single Market and the Stability Pact, the Frankfurt bankers (who are also unelected) can take any government to court for disregarding the Maastricht Treaty, while the Commission is now engaged in pursuing cases against the elected German and French governments for breaking the strict limits on public expenditure under the Stability Pact.

If the new European constitution comes into effect, other powers will pass from the parliaments we elect to the Council, Commission and Central Bank, and people here and everywhere in Europe will come to realise that whoever they vote for in national elections cannot change the laws that they are required to obey.

This is the most deadly threat to democracy and, if qualified majority voting removes the current veto system, any government could be outvoted and overruled and the people it was elected to represent would have no real say. Moreover, if the development of an independent foreign and defence policy takes place, we could be taken to war by decisions made elsewhere than in our own parliaments.

Not only is this a direct denial of democratic rights, but it removes the power of governments to discourage revolution or riot, on the grounds that a democratic solution is possible. Then the legitimacy and the stability of any political system come into question.

I am strongly in favour of European cooperation, having presented a bill for a Commonwealth of Europe that would include every country in our continent, as the basis for harmonisation by consent of the various parliaments, just as the UN General Assembly reaches agreements that it recommends should be followed.

The case for a European constitution and currency is also presented as a move beyond nationalism, which has brought such anguish to Europe. But I fear that it will stimulate nationalism when angry people discover that they are forced to do things they do not want to and are tempted to blame other nations, when the fault actually lies with the system itself.

Federations come and go, as we have seen in the Soviet Union and Yugoslavia, and I do not rule out the opportunity that the European Federation may break up amidst hostility between nations, which is the exact opposite of what we are told will happen.

4

A New Foreign and Defence Policy

Britain is now in effect an American colony, seen in Washington as an unsinkable aircraft carrier giving the US important military bases off the coast of Europe, and as a reliable political ally. British support permits what would otherwise be entirely unilateral actions to be presented as part of a 'coalition of the willing', purporting to be the international community around which the rest of the world has to revolve.

This came out clearly during the three most recent wars: in Yugoslavia, Afghanistan and Iraq, when London obediently followed the American lead and the 'special relationship' was defined by the Prime Minister as meaning that Britain has to be there 'when the shooting starts'.

To make this acceptable we were asked to believe something that was not true – namely that Saddam Hussein had weapons of mass destruction that could be mobilised in forty-five minutes and threaten world security. That lie has now been brushed aside by the simple statement that Iraq under the Ba'athists was a rogue state and we have liberated it by invading and occupying it.

As a part of this policy, Britain has abandoned its commitment to the Charter of the UN and now does what it is told by President Bush, just as it did for Clinton before him, when he bombed the Sudan, and for President Reagan when Margaret Thatcher was in Downing Street.

The American empire now spends more on defence than the next ten most powerful countries in the world put together. It was when Clinton was in the White House that his defence department issued a statement of its policy in crude and simple terms, calling for Full Spectrum Dominance, under which the United States would dominate the world in space, land, sea, air and information. This dominance reflected the thinking of those involved in drawing up the project for the new American century, guided by the neo-conservatives who are now responsible for American foreign policy and who are followed loyally by the Prime Minister, whose special relationship with President Bush is now the central feature of his thinking.

The language of imperialism invites us to accept that the US has a God-given right to run the world, and that the future of democracy and human rights depends on American missiles in space, their bombers, rockets and naval dominance. We in Britain are well placed to understand this because we were an empire ourselves.

In 1945 the British empire was on the eve of its final demise, partly because of the weakness of our economy, partly because of the rise of powerful liberation movements and partly because the post-war Labour government included those who had been brought up in the anti-imperialist tradition and who recognised the inevitable. They cooperated intelligently with the leaders of those colonies who wanted to be free, and thus avoided the folly and bloodshed that characterised the end of the French empire with the Algerian and Vietnam Wars.

My early years in Parliament involved me directly in many of these colonial and liberation movements. I had the privilege of knowing personally many of the leaders, including Gandhi and Nehru, Nkrumah, Cheddi Jagan, Kenneth Kaunda, Ben Bella and others, who had been imprisoned by the colonial powers as trouble-makers and terrorists and who ended up as heads of state, some having tea with the Queen as leader of the Commonwealth. I little thought at the time that at the end of my life I should see imperialism rise again and be embraced with such enthusiasm by Labour leaders now seeking power by piggybacking on top of a new empire possessing industrial, political, economic and military strength that we had lost.

Of course our relationship with the US began to develop under very different circumstances in two world wars and, without the attack on Pearl Harbor, President Roosevelt might have found it difficult in an isolationist America to take the US into the war. At that critical period we were glad to welcome American troops into Britain to mount the invasion of Europe from bases here.

But almost as soon as the war was over, the Cold War began and our Russian allies, who had borne the brunt of the German attack, were represented as a threat to our survival – a process that began with the use of atomic bombs at Hiroshima and Nagasaki, falsely justified as the only way to save American lives that would have been lost in a land invasion of Japan. In truth, the Japanese had already offered to surrender, provided that the Emperor was saved, which suited the Americans quite well since they feared that if the Emperor were to be displaced, Japan might become communist.

From 1945 until the fall of the Berlin Wall in 1989, the Cold War dominated the politics of Britain. It was the first rearmament programme launched in 1951 (over which Nye Bevan resigned) that weakened that post-war government and created the inflation that contributed to its defeat six months later. In his resignation speech, which I heard, Bevan dismissed the Soviet threat on three grounds: that the Soviet Union had no intention of attacking the West; that it did not have the military power to do so; and that it would lead to the very McCarthyism that later gripped the United States.

That rearmament programme also led us to divert essential resources from civil manufacture into military expenditure, which gravely weakened our economy while Germany and Japan, prohibited from rearmament, were able to concentrate their efforts on civil manufacture and eventually overtake Britain in exports.

The post-war Labour government took this decision under pressure from America and had earlier entered into arrangements with the US that were never revealed to Parliament, namely to accept permanent American air bases in Britain by explaining that they were part of US training missions, when in reality Attlee had secretly agreed to a long-term arrangement.

Attlee also concealed from Cabinet and Parliament his decision to build the atomic bomb for Britain – the UK having been a minor partner in the development of atomic weapons. Attlee considered that Britain too needed to have what became known as 'the deterrent', when we had the means of dropping those bombs by air.

When Britain adopted the American Polaris missile and

submarine system (now replaced by Trident), this locked us permanently into a dependence on the United States, since the technology was beyond the capacity of Aldermaston to provide and the global satellite guidance system was also under sole American control.

The establishment of NATO consolidated and concealed these arrangements because, of all the NATO countries, Britain was the only one that had some unofficial form of consultation with America, which supposedly requires them to notify us before the American bases here are used for operations. But, as we learned when America bombed Libya from Fairford in Gloucestershire, these consultations were never genuine and the arrangements themselves were never written down; I learned this from Fred Mulley, when he was Minister of Defence, who told me that they were simply reaffirmed orally by each incoming President and Prime Minister.

Thus Britain lost the power to act independently. This is the most important single feature of our defence and foreign policy, which is now locked – apparently irrevocably – into the White House and the Pentagon.

Field Marshal Carver, when he retired, said that over the centuries British military operations had been almost exclusively concerned with imperial expansion and colonial wars. It looks as if that situation has returned as part of our role as junior partner in the American global strategy to seek out 'rogue' states, remove their weapons of mass destruction and establish US bases around the world – now amounting to more than 740 bases in 134 countries.

In that sense, New Labour is firmly unilateralist in its attitude towards nuclear weapons, so long as unilateralism is imposed on the 'rogue' states and cannot under any circumstances be applied to Britain, with our weapons of mass destruction under American control.

Now that the Soviet Union has disappeared, American power is reaching into the heart of the old USSR, partly to guarantee the supply of Caspian oil to the West and partly as a long-term strategy for the encirclement of China, which, before this century is halfway through, will be as powerful as the United States. Communists have now been replaced by Muslim fundamentalists as the enemy – the same Muslim fundamentalists who, during the height of the Soviet empire, America was arming as its allies in fighting communism; as when Osama bin Laden was funded and armed to get Soviet troops out of Afghanistan.

The emergence of plans for an extended European union, with its own defence force capable of acting independently if the need arose, has caused some anxiety in Washington, and is only hesitantly supported by New Labour for that reason. The policy is based on the totally illusory idea that the new Europe could in some way be a rival to, and a check on, the all-powerful United States.

The one question that is never asked or seriously discussed in Britain is whether this new defence and foreign policy is the right one for this country to follow. Or whether we should be thinking of a totally different policy, based on a non-nuclear Britain, without US bases, with Britain using its influence (both political and military) to strengthen the United Nations, which desperately needs support to prevent it being sidetracked and virtually destroyed by American power. In 2003 the UN was brushed aside by the Anglo-American decision to launch a pre-emptive war against Iraq in defiance of the Charter.

A new purpose to make real the hopes of the founders of the

UN Charter, the declaration of human rights and UNESCO, and the relief of poverty is so exciting for a younger generation, and for me. It would be far more likely to make the world a safer place than would Star Wars and a huge nuclear arsenal, which could not protect the Twin Towers against suicide bombers.

I have never been a pacifist, but I do believe in the peaceful settlement of international disputes, which is how 'pacifism' is described in the *Oxford English Dictionary*. Having lived through the Blitz, I know how frightening an air bombardment is. And I bitterly resent the way in which the media and politicians use war to boost their power and popularity, when the real problems of humanity remain neglected, because of the money and skill poured into dangerous and irrelevant arms programmes.

That is why the world peace movement that organised the massive demonstrations across the globe in the last few years offers the best hope for the future of humanity and deserves our support. This is a view widely shared by younger people, who understandably do not believe what they are told about the threats we face or the policies we are instructed to follow in order to deal with them.

These are the issues my children and grandchildren will have to face. And, in my considered view, that is the only rational way to proceed.

5

Peace

*My hatred of war and passion for peace and justice I first learned
at home. But they became stronger as a result of my own
experience, living through a world war and witnessing many others
since 1945. The arguments for just wars, and the supposed merits
of globalised capitalism, form the basis of a political consensus
that infects virtually all media coverage. That consensus must be
challenged if the human race is to survive.*

HOUSE OF COMMONS DEBATE ON THE GULF WAR, 6 SEPTEMBER 1990

Many hon. Members have said that this is the gravest crisis that
we have faced since 1945, and I share that view . . . There has
been a demand – quite properly in a crisis – for a degree of unity,
and that unity has been present in a number of important respects.
No hon. Member supports the act of aggression by Saddam
Hussein against Kuwait. So far as I know, no hon. Member is other

than strongly supportive of the sanctions taken by the United Nations against Saddam Hussein and the resolution for their enforcement. We also have something else in common – none of us will be killed if a war breaks out.

But as Members of Parliament, we have responsibilities which cannot simply be subordinated to the role of the government. This is not the place to deal with it, but under our constitution, military deployments, acts of war and treaties of peace come under the Crown prerogative. Parliament has no legal or constitutional right whatever to decide the matters that are before us for debate.

But we have a duty to represent people. We have a duty to represent – as far as I can make out, some Conservative Members have done it with tremendous energy – British citizens in Iraq and Kuwait. We have a responsibility for them and their families. That has hardly been mentioned except as an instrument for denouncing, quite properly, the man who is detaining them. We have service men and women in the Middle East, and perhaps more are to go there if the stories in today's papers are right. They and their families are entitled to have Members of Parliament to represent them. There are the refugees, thousands of them without water and food, and as human beings we have a responsibility to them. I might add that the tragic pictures that we have seen of people in the desert, without proper food or shelter, would be as nothing to what would happen if war broke out. As you know, Mr Speaker, because we discussed it yesterday, I intend to oppose the motion tomorrow that the House should now adjourn. This is the one rare occasion when whether we should adjourn for another six weeks while events take their course is the real question . . . I remind the House that on 5 May 1940, when Hitler was at the gates, there was an adjournment debate on the handling by the government of the Campaign in Norway, and a vote. The then Prime Minister [Neville Chamberlain] won the vote and resigned, and Winston Churchill became Prime Minister. So let us not be told that the duty of the House of Commons is to unite behind whatever the government of the day does, because that is not what the House is there to do. We are here to represent people and to contribute our own opinions as best we can. I have no complaint of any speech made today about how we feel that the crisis should be handled.

I will use plain language. I fear that the United States has already decided that, when it is ready, it will create a pretext for a war. That is what I believe. I acquit the Foreign Secretary of being in that hawkish clan because, in so far as one can penetrate the inscrutable corridors of power and the minds of their inhabitants, he seems to be a bit of a dove. But let me say this, too, without offence. Britain is a minor player in this game. We have had a debate today as though everything hinged on whether the Prime Minister decided to go to war. The Prime Minister, too, is a minor player in this unfolding tragedy. She decided to go in with President Bush, perhaps because of the transatlantic relationship, the so-called 'special relationship', or as thanks for the Falklands, or because she did not want to get mixed up with the EEC.

But she is a minor player, and once she and the Cabinet decided to commit even a notional number of forces – including the RAF and the RAF Regiment and now the troops – she was locked into what President Bush intended to do. It is important that we should not discuss, as if we were in a position to decide the post-Cold War order, what the Prime Minister will be doing here and there. We are a minor partner in an American strategy.

It must be known by now that I am opposed to a war against

Iraq. I am opposed to action outside the United Nations. I believe that it would divide the Security Council. It might not exactly unite the Arab world, but it might bring many Arab countries together against us. The outcome of such a war could not be sure, because President Saddam Hussein would certainly have the capacity, were he to choose to do it, to destroy so many oil installations that, even though he himself might be destroyed, it would inflict a burden on the world economy and the Middle East which could not be contemplated . . .

Governments of any colour in any country are not the main practitioners of morality. America went into Panama and 3,000 people were killed. America went into Grenada. America supported Iraq when it attacked Iran. America did nothing when Cyprus was invaded and partitioned by Turkey. America has no moral authority, any more than any other super-power. The same would be true of the Soviet Union after Afghanistan, or wherever. It has no moral authority. Nor, might I add, because these things must be said and nobody else has said them, can we defend the Emir or the King of Saudi Arabia, neither of whom practise any democracy. I am not saying that they are not entitled to the protection of the UN Charter – I have already said that they are – but, given the denunciations of the breaches of human rights in Eastern Europe by ministers, one might have expected one of them, in this dispute, to point out that a person found guilty of shoplifting in Riyadh will have his hand chopped off. Are we to live in a world where morality is seen as the product of a parliamentary majority?

The real issue is this. Everybody knows it and nobody has mentioned it. The Americans want to protect their oil supplies . . . The former Attorney-General of the United States, Ramsey

Clark, said on the radio last night that the United States forced Saudi Arabia to accept its army there because it wanted to protect its oil.

We are experienced as an imperial power and that will not shock the Conservatives. I am not asking anyone to be shocked, only to recognise the fact that stares us in the face. America has benefited much recently from cheap Middle Eastern oil. It was reported in the *Financial Times* that it has reduced its oil production and increased its oil imports from 31 per cent to 52 per cent. It has become hooked on this cheap fluid that now has to be controlled by the American army. That is honestly the position. The United States wants a permanent base . . .

Then there is the arms trade. That has been brought out a bit. A couple of years ago, in Algiers, I met a former Egyptian Foreign Minister who told me that there had been a seminar in Cairo about the Crusades and that, during the Crusades, European arms manufacturers supplied arms both to Richard Coeur de Lion and to Saladin. Nothing has really changed. Arms manufacturers have made billions of pounds from selling instruments of mass destruction, partly to hold down those colonial people so that the sheikhs will supply cheap oil, and partly because it is highly profitable to sell arms. I shall not try to differentiate between governments, because the Labour government did it too . . .

The arms trade is a corrupt trade. If our troops have to fight those of Saddam Hussein – I hope that that does not happen – they will be fighting against modern weapons in part sold by Britain, France, America and Russia for profit. That is a major issue.

If we go to war – and there are those who think that we might – what will be our war aims? That is not an unreasonable question.

Will it be to free Kuwait, to topple Hussein, or to destroy Iraqi weapons? My right hon. Friend the Leader of the Opposition [Neil Kinnock] went further than the Prime Minister in setting the objective. She said that it was to arrest Saddam Hussein and to bring him before an international crimes tribunal. The Prime Minister said that on television. Are British troops to be sent in to fight before their objective has been clarified? The government have never made clear what is their aim. However, it is clear that the United States, having helped to arm Hussein, is determined to bring him down and to establish a new base.

I do not need to dwell on the consequences of war. They include a massive loss of life and possibly an air attack on oil installations. In the peculiar circumstances, we would to some extent, if not in every sense, be taking on Islam. There are 105 million Muslims in India alone.

The Prime Minister courteously gave way to me when I asked what I hope was a relevant question. She said three times – so she must have meant it – that she already has the legal right to attack Iraq and that no further stages are necessary. The only consideration is that that will be done not at her discretion, but at that of President Bush. I say to my right hon. Friend the Leader of the Opposition that anyone who goes into the Lobby with the government tomorrow night will be endorsing the view that no further action is needed to legalise an attack on Iraq.

Those who vote with the government tomorrow will be voting for giving the Prime Minister a free hand or a blank cheque. Those who vote against the government will be accepting the view expressed in my early-day motion, which calls on the government 'to make a clear and unequivocal statement that it will not commit British Forces to offensive military operations against Iraq that have not been explicitly authorised by a Resolution passed by the Security Council, and under the provisions of the UN Charter, which deal with the use of force by the United Nations and under its military command' . . .

There has been a 7 per cent fall in oil production worldwide but a 100 per cent increase in its price. How is that justified? Thank God for Winston Churchill, who in 1914, when he was First Lord of the Admiralty, nationalised the Anglo-Iranian Petroleum Company for £2 million. His speech on that occasion made the strongest case for public control and ownership of oil companies that one can find. Winston Churchill said that countries were being squeezed by the oil companies.

If there is to be a peace-keeping force, it would be better if it were Arab, but I turn to the longer, post-Cold War perspective, to which our attention has been properly drawn by a number of speeches. One cannot have a new order for the Middle East based on the redeployment of white power in the form of a permanent American army in Saudi Arabia. That will not work. One is no longer dealing with the natives who featured in Rudyard Kipling's poems, but with a quite different world. For me, the United Nations is the General Assembly, not the bigwigs, permanent and rotating members who sit on the Security Council. I personally would like to see direct elections to the General Assembly. They might only return one British Member of Parliament, but I would certainly be a candidate, if that were possible.

We are always being told that we must come to terms with reality and that we must not live in the past. The fact remains that we live in a very small world of many religions. There are fundamentalist Christians. When President Reagan spoke of an evil empire, he was declaring a Christian jihad against communism. Anyone

who has visited America and listened to those Christian fundamentalists, who have not got into trouble and been removed, will
know that they make their reputations out of their religious wars
against communism. However, as right hon. and hon. Members
know very well, the Americans stimulated Islam to defeat communism – but when communism changed, fundamentalism remained.

We shall have to plan and share the world's oil. America has
only 2 per cent of the world's population, but uses 25 per cent of
the world's resources. That situation cannot be allowed to last,
even if America has a big army. The real function of the United
Nations is to act as the custodian of social justice. It should not
serve just as a policeman . . . I urge caution, because many other
Western European nations are being very cautious and have not
sent troops. Many of the non-aligned countries are not really
behind the action being taken by America and Britain. It is time
to try to take some of the hatred out of the situation . . .

I urge caution because it is not the hardware of military weapons
that frightens me. A gun cannot go off by itself. It is the hatred
which makes people want to use weapons. That is the fuel of war
and in the past few months we have had the most vicious war
propaganda pumped down our throats. The temper of peace, of
which Pandit Nehru used to speak, is what we need, and we want
to be cautious and to let it work its way through the United
Nations.

HOUSE OF COMMONS DEBATE ON NUCLEAR DEFENCE,
14 JANUARY 1992

When the election comes, I shall present myself to the people
of Chesterfield as a candidate who is committed to the ending of

nuclear weapons and bases in Britain. I shall do that because that is what I put to the electors in 1987 and 1984. I resigned from the Front Bench in 1958 because I could not support a policy of using nuclear weapons. That is my position . . .

At the end of the Cold War, it is necessary for those of us who take the view that I take to restate our position, given contemporary circumstances . . .

When I listened to the Secretary of State's [Tom King's] arguments, I became even more convinced of the rightness of what I have been saying. The Soviet Union had nuclear weapons on a huge scale, but they did not protect the Soviet Union. It collapsed. Indeed, it collapsed partly because it had wasted so much money on nuclear weapons, but I shall return to that point in a moment. Nuclear weapons do not guarantee the integrity of a state against either internal or external enemies.

If it is really true that some nuclear weapons are now in the hands of hungry, riotous and underpaid soldiers and are being serviced by nuclear scientists who are not receiving any money, what effect can a British deterrent have? Those people probably do not have sufficient communications to know of the existence of such a deterrent.

I put it to the Secretary of State that it was the policy of the West to bankrupt the Soviet Union . . . The fact is that the Soviet Union was bankrupted by its military expenditure. That, more than anything else, probably explains why changes have occurred in the Soviet Union. I hope that no one thinks that what has happened in the Soviet Union happened because people in Moscow went around whispering to each other, 'The British government are ordering Trident: we had better abandon communism.' That had nothing to do with what happened. The Soviet people wanted freedom. What happened had nothing to do with the threat from the West.

I must say something else so that it is put on the record before it passes into history. The Western intelligence agents used Islam to undermine communism . . .

We are also told that it is wicked for Russian scientists to leave the Soviet Union to get more money elsewhere. I thought that that was what market forces are all about. The Conservative Party says that one cannot interfere with market forces, but if a Russian scientist goes to Tehran to work on nuclear matters, Conservative Members say that that must be stopped – if necessary by having more Trident missiles. What nonsense the whole business is.

Turning to arms sales, are we not the world's second-largest arms exporter? But if the Russians cannot get enough food and sell a few weapons to buy food, Conservative Members say that that must be stopped.

I fear that at the end of this period we shall see a repetition of the Gulf War – against Libya and Cuba and, possibly, the toppling of Castro and Gaddafi – because the Soviet Union's weakness has led the Americans to believe that they can run the world. That is what the new world order is about.

Mr Viggers [Conservative Member for Gosport]: The whole House respects the integrity of the right hon. Gentleman, who is a signatory to the amendment tabled by the hon. Member for Islington, North [Mr Corbyn]. How many of his hon. Friends does the right hon. Gentleman think will put before their electors the clear policy that he intends to put before the voters of Chesterfield? How many Labour Members and Labour candidates does the right hon. Gentleman think would support the amendment that has been tabled by his hon. Friend the Member for Islington, North?

Does the right hon. Gentleman regard himself – I say this in a friendly manner – as something of a political dodo?

Mr Benn: My position is unilateralist and always has been. The hon. Gentleman has asked a very silly question because a substantial number of people in this country share my view – far more than might be suggested by the number of their parliamentary representatives. Let us start with the argument that the Cold War was ended by the nuclear deterrent and that we did not have a war because of that deterrent. It was not until I went to Hiroshima that I learned that, far from the bomb being dropped there to bring the Japanese to the peace table, they had offered to surrender weeks before. The bomb was dropped on Hiroshima to tell the Russians that we had such a weapon. That all came out at the war-crimes tribunals in Japan.

I have never had any sympathy with the Soviet system and its lack of democracy, but I never believed that the Russians were threatening to invade Western Europe. Like, I am sure, most people in this country, I never believed that. Does anyone honestly think that the Russians, with all their domestic problems, planned to take over West Germany, Italy and France and come to London to 'deal with Ken Livingstone' or go to Northern Ireland to 'deal with Ian Paisley'? Does anyone honestly think that that was their strategy? That threat was the most convenient political instrument ever used in domestic politics because those who criticised the Conservative government were regarded as agents of the KGB.

Indeed, when the Secretary of State for Defence talks about the Campaign for Nuclear Disarmament, he ought to know. His Department ordered the bugging of CND and treated its members, who were honest, decent people, as though they were enemies of the state. Cathy Massiter resigned from MI5 because she would not go along with its KGB tactics. So of course the Secretary of State knows a lot about CND. He probably knows a lot about what we say to each other on our telephones today. I hope that he does, because my telephone is the only remaining link that I have with the British establishment. So I speak clearly and I hope that those who are listening understand what I am saying.

The second argument against nuclear weapons is that we cannot afford them . . . When we look back at the reasons why the British economy has been weak in the past forty years, one of the main ones is that we have wasted too much money on weapons of war that are not necessary.

I think that I am right in saying that six out of ten scientists in Britain still work on defence or in defence-related industries. Let us consider the country which now has the most powerful nuclear arsenal in the world – America. Bush has to go to Japan to plead with the Japanese to buy a few more gas-guzzlers from Detroit. Why is Japan so rich? Because it has not wasted all that money on nuclear and other weapons. Neither have the Germans. We would not let them do so at the beginning. But the shops are full of Japanese cameras, videos, cars and Japanese this-and-that. All that we can offer to sell is a few missiles to a sheikh. That is our major export drive as a major arms supplier. We cannot afford those weapons. That is a powerful reason for not having them.

The third argument against nuclear weapons is that they do not deter anyone. Has anyone re-examined the deterrent argument? Argentina attacked a nuclear state – Britain – when it went into the Falklands. Did nuclear weapons deter Galtieri? Not on your life. He knew that we could not use them against him. Saddam Hussein defied an ultimatum from two nuclear states – the United States and Britain. Did nuclear weapons deter him?

Not on your life. He dropped some Scuds on another nuclear state – Israel. Did nuclear weapons deter him? Not on your life. The whole deterrent argument is a fraud . . .

I now come to another point, and perhaps I may put on another hat. I was the minister responsible for Aldermaston from 1966 to 1970. Like most people, I have had a chequered career. We do not have our own nuclear weapons. Since the Vulcan and the early bombs, we have depended on the Americans. Aldermaston may not even be able – I do not claim inside knowledge; if I had it, I would not speak in this way – to refurbish the weapons that the Americans give us. We do not have a nuclear deterrent, and if we did, we could not use it without the American worldwide satellite network which provides communication.

The Labour Party was never unilateralist in Parliament. I challenge anyone to find one motion tabled in the House of Commons in which the Labour Front Bench advocated unilateralism. It simply talked about it at conference and then came back and did nothing about it. But can anyone imagine a more absurd democratic fiasco than that there should be election after election in which we discuss whether we should, or should not, have what we do not have anyway?

I tell the House solemnly one thing that the Americans would do. If Boris Yeltsin said, 'I will take my nuclear weapons away from the Ukraine if you will take them away from Britain', the Americans would be wise to do so, because the Ukraine is more of a threat than Britain. The Americans could take our weapons away simply by cutting off the supply.

My last point is dear to my heart. Simply having nuclear weapons destroys democracy. When a country has them, ministers – of all parties – lie. No minister has ever told the truth about any central question of nuclear policy. We heard that today. We were told that the government could not say when they would use nuclear weapons. If we ask whether they exist in any one location, the government say that they cannot confirm or deny it. Every party has done the same. I am not making a party point. Mr Attlee built the atom bomb without telling Parliament.

Of course, any leader of a Third World country who reads the speech of the Secretary of State for Defence will be able to use it in his own assembly to say, 'If the British say that, it must be right for Iran, Libya and everywhere else.' The Secretary of State made the most powerful case for nuclear proliferation. We are proliferating with Trident. It represents a major addition to our armoury. Britain is a small country, but we have such pretensions – we speak as though we were a super-power. We are a tiny country, and the idea that our deterrent will somehow determine whether Kazakhstan will agree to inspection is misleading. If one continues misleading people, in the end it will catch up with one. That is what Russia learned. It is time that we came to terms with the fact that we are a small island off the west coast of Europe. We depend on a new association across the whole of Europe . . . We should bring countries into a pan-European association rather than building up our own weapons, which is what the Liberal Party has policies for. We must seek political solutions to problems which we are still told are best dealt with by military means.

HOUSE OF COMMONS DEBATE ON THE SITUATION IN IRAQ, 17 FEBRUARY 1998

No one in the House supports the regime of Saddam Hussein, who is a brutal dictator. Secondly, no one in the House can defend for one moment the denial by the Iraqi government of the implementation of the Security Council resolution which said that there should be inspections. The third issue on which there is major agreement, but little understanding yet, is the sudden realisation of the horror of modern chemical and biological weapons, which do not depend on enormous amounts of hardware – previously only available to a super-power – but which almost anybody, perhaps even a terrorist group, could deliver.

The disagreement is on how we deal with the matter. The former Prime Minister, the right hon. Member for Huntingdon [John Major] – whose speech was listened to with great attention – was talking about a preventive war. I shall read Hansard carefully, but he talked about a preventive war. There is no provision in the UN charter for a preventive war. If we are realistic – we must not fool ourselves – that huge American fleet of 30 ships and 1,000 aircraft is not in the Gulf waiting to be withdrawn when Saddam makes a friendly noise to Kofi Annan. The fleet has been sent there to be used, and the House would be deceiving itself if it thought that any so-called 'diplomatic initiatives' would avert its use.

This is a unique debate as far as I am concerned. I have sat here with the right hon. Member for Old Bexley and Sidcup [Sir Edward Heath] through four wars – the Korean War, the Suez War, the Falklands War and the first Gulf War. I cannot remember an occasion when any government asked the House to authorise, in a resolution, action which could lead to force.

The reason is that the right to go to war is a prerogative power. The government are inviting the House – I understand why – to share their responsibility for the use of force, *knowing* that force will be used within a week or two.

We are not starting afresh. I opposed the Gulf War. We should have asked why Saddam got into Kuwait and why he was not stopped. We had the war. The equivalent of seven and a half Hiroshima bombs was dropped on the people of Iraq – the biggest bombardment since the Second World War. Some 200,000 Iraqis died. Depleted uranium bullets were used. I have had two or three letters from Gulf War veterans in a mass of correspondence in the past week, one of whom has offered to be a human shield in Iraq because he feels that he was betrayed by the British government and does not want the Iraqi people to suffer again.

All the evidence confirms my view that sanctions are another instrument of mass destruction. They destroy people's lives, denying them the food and medicines that they need. It is no good saying that Saddam took the money for his palaces. If that is the case, why does the United Nations Children's Fund now say that there are one million children in Iraq starving, along with 500,000 who have died?

Bombing the water supply and the sewerage plants is like using chemical weapons, because the disease that spreads from that bombing contributes to disease in the country. And, at the end of all that, Saddam is stronger than he was at the beginning. Nobody denies that. People ask why we have to go back seven years later. It is because the previous policy inevitably made him stronger. We know that when a country is attacked, leaders wave their fists and say, 'We will never give way.' It happened in Britain, it happens when we are dealing with bombings from Ireland – it happens all the time. Are we such fools that we think that if we bomb other people they will crumble, whereas when they bomb us it will stiffen our resolve? The House ought to study its own history.

The government's motion would not be carried at the Security Council. I asked the Foreign Secretary [Robin Cook] about that. Why is he asking us to pass a resolution that he could not get through the Security Council? On the basis of his speech, the Russians and the Chinese would not vote for the use of force. Why involve the House of Commons in an act that runs counter to what the Security Council would accept?

I hope that the House will listen to me. I know that my view is not the majority view in the House, although it may be outside this place.

I regret that I shall vote against the government motion. The first victims of the bombing that I believe will be launched within a fortnight will be innocent people, many, if not most, of whom would like Saddam to be removed. The former Prime Minister, the right hon. Member for Huntingdon, talked about collateral damage. The military men are clever. They talk not about hydrogen bombs but about deterrence. They talk not about people but about collateral damage. They talk not about power stations and sewerage plants but about assets. The reality is that innocent people will be killed if the House votes tonight – as it manifestly will – to give the government the authority for military action.

The bombing would also breach the United Nations charter. I do not want to argue on legal terms. If the hon. and learned Member for North-East Fife [Menzies Campbell] has read articles 41 and 42, he will know that the charter says that military action can only be decided on by the Security Council and conducted under the military staffs committee. That procedure has not been followed and cannot be followed because the five permanent members have to agree. Even for the Korean War, the United States had to go to the General Assembly to get authority because

Russia was absent. That was held to be a breach, but at least an overwhelming majority was obtained.

Has there been any negotiation or diplomatic effort? Why has the Foreign Secretary not been in Baghdad, like the French Foreign Minister, the Turkish Foreign Minister and the Russian Foreign Minister? The time that the government said that they wanted for negotiation has been used to prepare public opinion for war and to build up their military position in the Gulf.

Saddam will be strengthened again. Or he may be killed. I read today that the security forces – who are described as terrorists in other countries – have tried to kill Saddam. I should not be surprised if they succeeded.

This second action does not enjoy support from elsewhere. There is no support from Iraq's neighbours. If what the Foreign Secretary says about the threat to the neighbours is true, why is Iran against, why is Jordan against, why is Saudi Arabia against, why is Turkey against? Where is that great support? There is no support from the opposition groups inside Iraq. The Kurds, the Shi'ites and the communists hate Saddam, but they do not want the bombing. The Pope is against it, along with ten bishops, two cardinals, Boutros Boutros-Ghali and Perez de Cuellar. The Foreign Secretary clothes himself with the garment of the world community, but he does not have that support. We are talking about an Anglo-American preventive war. It has been planned and we are asked to authorise it in advance.

The House is clear about its view of history, but it does not say much about the history of the areas with which we are dealing. The borders of Kuwait and Iraq, which then became sacrosanct, were drawn by the British after the end of the Ottoman empire. We used chemical weapons against the Iraqis in the 1930s. Air

Chief Marshal Harris, who later flattened Dresden, was instructed to drop chemical weapons.

When Saddam came to power, he was a hero of the West. The Americans used him against Iran because they hated Khomeini, who was then the figure to be removed.

They armed Saddam, used him and sent him anthrax. I am not anxious to make a party political point, because there is not much difference between the two sides on this, but, as the Scott report revealed, the previous government allowed him to be armed. I had three hours with Saddam in 1990. I got the hostages out, which made it worth going. He felt betrayed by the United States, because the American Ambassador in Baghdad had said to him, 'If you go into Kuwait, we will treat it as an Arab matter.' That is part of the history that they know, even if we do not know it here.

In 1958, forty years ago, Selwyn Lloyd, the Foreign Secretary and later the Speaker, told Foster Dulles that Britain would make Kuwait a Crown colony. Foster Dulles said, 'What a very good idea.' We may not know that history, but in the Middle East it is known.

The Conservatives have tabled an amendment asking about the objectives. That is an important issue. There is no UN resolution saying that Saddam must be toppled. It is not clear that the government know what their objectives are. They will probably be told from Washington. Do they imagine that if we bomb Saddam for two weeks, he will say, 'Oh, by the way, do come in and inspect'? The plan is misconceived.

Some hon. Members – even Opposition Members – have pointed out the double standard. I am not trying to equate Israel with Iraq, but on 8 June 1981, Israel bombed a nuclear reactor near Baghdad. What action did either party take on that? Israel is in breach of UN resolutions and has instruments of mass destruction. Mordecai Vanunu would not boast about Israeli freedom. Turkey breached UN resolutions by going into northern Cyprus. It has also recently invaded northern Iraq and has instruments of mass destruction. Lawyers should know better than anyone else that it does not matter whether we are dealing with a criminal thug or an ordinary lawbreaker – if the law is to apply, it must apply to all. Governments of both major parties have failed in that.

Prediction is difficult and dangerous, but I fear that the situation could end in a tragedy for the American and British governments. Suez and Vietnam are not far from the minds of anyone with a sense of history . . . If the Kurds are free, they will demand Kurdistan and destabilise Turkey. Anything could happen. We are sitting here as if we still had an empire – only, fortunately, we have a bigger brother with more weapons than us.

The British government have everything at their disposal. They are permanent members of the Security Council and have the European Union presidency for six months. Where is that leadership in Europe which we were promised? It just disappeared. We are also, of course, members of the Commonwealth, in which there are great anxieties. We have thrown away our influence, which could have been used for moderation.

The amendment that I and others have tabled argues that the United Nations Security Council should decide the nature of what Kofi Annan brings back from Baghdad and whether force is to be used. Inspections and sanctions go side by side. As I said, sanctions are brutal for innocent people. Then there is the real question: when will the world come to terms with the fact that chemical weapons are available to anybody? If there is an answer to that, it must involve the most meticulous observation of international law, which I feel we are abandoning.

War is easy to talk about; there are not many people left of the generation which remembers it. The right hon. Member for Old Bexley and Sidcup [Sir Edward Heath] served with distinction in the last war. I never killed anyone, but I wore uniform. I was in London during the Blitz in 1940, living where the Millbank Tower now stands, where I was born. Some different ideas have come in there since. Every night, I went to the shelter in Thames House. Every morning, I saw docklands burning. Five hundred people were killed in Westminster one night by a land mine. It was terrifying. Are not Arabs and Iraqis terrified? Do not Arab and Iraqi women weep when their children die? Does not bombing strengthen their determination? What fools we are to live as if war is a computer game for our children or just an interesting little Channel 4 news item.

Every Member of Parliament who votes for the government motion will be consciously and deliberately accepting responsibility for the deaths of innocent people if the war begins, as I fear it will. That decision is for every hon. Member to take. In my parliamentary experience, this a unique debate. We are being asked to share responsibility for a decision that we will not really be taking, but which will have consequences for people who have no part to play in the brutality of the regime with which we are dealing.

On 24 October 1945 – the right hon. Member for Old Bexley and Sidcup will remember – the United Nations Charter was passed. The words of that charter are etched on my mind and move me even as I think of them. It says:

> We the peoples of the United Nations determined to save succeeding generations from the scourge of war, which twice in our lifetime has brought untold sorrow to mankind . . .

That was that generation's pledge to this generation, and it would be the greatest betrayal of all if we voted to abandon the charter, take unilateral action and pretend that we were doing so in the name of the international community. I shall vote against the motion for the reasons that I have given.

HOUSE OF COMMONS DEBATE ON THE WORLD TRADE ORGANISATION, 9 DECEMBER 1999

This debate was arranged to celebrate another triumph for free trade, and it has turned out to be a long overdue – and, in my case, very welcome – debate about the real nature of global capitalism. It is from that point of view that I want to address the House.

Free trade and global capitalism are accepted almost unanimously among important people in Britain. Multinational companies demand free trade because it gives them freedom. The City needs it to prosper as a financial centre. Speculators depend on it. Most newspaper proprietors and editors are committed to it. The BBC is so devout about free trade that it broadcasts share values and currency values every hour, entirely replacing the daily prayer service. Teachers explain free trade in business-study courses, and some trade-union leaders believe that free trade is bound to come about.

All Front-Bench Members are utterly committed to global capitalism and free trade. Conservative Members, whether pro or anti the single currency, are utterly committed to capitalism. The Liberals, with their Gladstonian tradition and the Manchester school, are committed to capitalism. I say with the greatest respect that I have never heard a more powerful speech for world capitalism than that just made by my right hon. Friend the Secretary of State for Trade and Industry [Stephen Byers], who occupies an office that I once held.

Third-way philosophers line up to support capitalism and free trade. Modernisers and focus groups yearn for more of it, and business-friendly ministers think of nothing else. Labour Members had an important letter from four Department of Trade and Industry ministers on 24 November, and the contents of that letter were reproduced in the minister's speech.

The truth is that the benefits of capitalism and free trade are not really being seen in the world at all. We are told, for example, that the best way to narrow the gap between rich and poor is to have free trade and world capitalism. Ten years ago, the world had 147 dollar billionaires; five years ago, it had 274 dollar billionaires, and that number increased recently to 447. Those billionaires have a combined wealth equivalent to the annual income of half of the world's population.

We must consider also what the World Health Organisation says about the health of the world. One-fifth of the world's children live in poverty; one-third of the world's children are undernourished, and half of the world's population lack access to essential drugs. Each year, twelve million children under five die, and 95 per cent of them die from poverty-related illness; more than half a million mothers die in childbirth, and more than one million babies die of tetanus. What contribution have globalisation and free trade made to solving those problems? The theory that wealth trickles down and that the richer Bill Gates gets, the richer people in Asia will get, is one of the most ludicrous illusions that could possibly be imagined.

What the Secretary of State did not say is that the one thing that globalisation has done is to make multinational companies more powerful than countries. That is why so many Third World countries are worried. Fifty-one of the largest 100 economies in the world are now corporations: Mitsubishi's is bigger than that of Indonesia; General Motors's is bigger than that of Denmark; Ford's is bigger than that of South Africa; and Toyota's is bigger than that of Norway. The sales of the top 200 corporations are greater than one-quarter of the world's economic activity.

Multinational corporations want free trade because they are trying to get governments off their back so that they can exploit the profits that they can make with the minimum of interference. They think that global capitalism and free trade will end redistributive taxation and, although this has not been mentioned so far, gradually turn health and education into market-related activities.

A restricted paper circulated to World Trade Organisation delegates was brought to my attention by one of the Members of the European Parliament who received it. It asked, 'How can WTO members ensure that ongoing reforms in national health systems are mutually supportive and whenever relevant market-based?'

It will not be long before some countries can say to others, 'You are discriminating against us because you have a health service and our workers have not, so you must cut back your health service so that you are not taking unfair advantage.'

The Secretary of State for International Development [Clare Short]: There are many myths about the WTO, partly because the negotiations are so complicated that people can make up anything that they like. There is an agreement on trade in services. Some developing countries need banking and other financial services to get their economies going, but the agreement says that each country will open whatever sectors it wants to the market, and there is no compulsion for it to open any sector that it does not want to open.

Mr Benn: There may be no compulsion, but the WTO would like health to be market-related.

Clare Short: No, that is not true.

Mr Benn: Well, it said so in the document, and my right hon. Friend must have seen it.

This is a debate marking the end of the millennium, and I do not want to get into a party argument at all; I want to try to understand what is happening. Not long ago, Richard Whelan from the Institute of Economic Affairs said, 'Africa should be privatised and leases to run individual countries auctioned off.'

That is serious. In the *Financial Times*, James Morgan, the BBC economics correspondent, said:

If some countries, especially in Africa, were to be run along the lines of commercial enterprises rather than states, investors might find them much more attractive.

That is what the multinational companies are thinking about. When the Secretary of State drew a comparison with the Luddites, he reminded me of the leading article in *The Economist* on 26 February 1848 – a year or two before I entered the House – in which the slave trade was discussed. The article said:

222

If in place of entering into Treaties for the suppression of the Slave Trade, we made conventions to ameliorate the conditions of the existing race of slaves – to establish and regulate on unquestionable principles the free emigration of Africans . . . we might, with a tenth of the cost, do a great substantial good to the African Race.

I can imagine Ofslave being set up, with Chris Woodhead in charge, naming and shaming the captains of slave ships on which the sanitary arrangements for slaves are inadequate. For God's sake, surely we must take some account in this debate of the worry of the enormous number of people in the world who have not got rich through free trade.

Global capitalism empowers companies to move money freely, but it does not allow workers to move freely. If someone owns a factory in London, but the wages are so high that he cannot make a profit, he can close it and open it in Malaysia, where wages are lower. If, however, someone from Malaysia tries to come to London where wages are higher, immigration laws would keep him out.

Globalisation has nothing to do with internationalism. At least in the European Union there is a free movement of capital and labour. We are not talking about letting workers move in search of higher wages, but only of companies moving in search of higher profits. Global capitalism allows big business to run the banana republics. It involves risks to the protection of the environment, and we are told that it is inevitable.

We have had free trade in Britain for a long time, but it has not solved the problems of poverty automatically. There was terrible poverty in Dickensian Britain and, even today, the gap between rich and poor is wider, even though Yorkshire cannot impose bans or tariffs on goods from Derbyshire . . .

Let us look at the matter from another point of view that is all the more important. Global capital is eroding political democracy. Power has already been transferred to Eddie George [Governor of the Bank of England]. I do not know which constituency he won at the election; I could not find his name anywhere on the list. None the less, he has more power than the Chancellor of the Exchequer. The European Central Bank will have more power than either of them.

None of the representatives of the International Monetary Fund, the World Bank and the WTO is elected. Who elects the Secretary-General of NATO and the Director-General of the WTO? Nobody. Our political democracy has been decapitated in the interests of worship of money. As Keir Hardie said at the beginning of the century, we must choose between worshipping God or Mammon, and there is no doubt on which we decided.

That brings me to another matter. People outside the House know that there is a massive coalition in this Parliament in favour of capitalism, and they are therefore becoming cynical and disillusioned with the political process. One of the reasons why people do not vote is that they think that there is one view inside the House – that all the leaders are huddling together in coalitions and patriotic alliances – and that they are excluded from it.

The minister who made that point clear [Peter Mandelson] is now the Secretary of State for Northern Ireland. He said in Bonn on 3 March last year, 'It may be that the era of pure representative democracy is coming slowly to an end.' That was a more candid account of what is happening than the praise of trade in this debate.

The Prime Minister [Tony Blair], if I may quote him with approval, said when Leader of the Opposition during a debate on the Halifax summit in June 1995, 'Is not the central issue the revolution in the globalisation of the financial and currency markets, which now wield massive speculative power over the governments of all countries and have the capacity seriously to disrupt economic progress?' [*Official Report*, 19 June 1995; vol. 262, c. 23–4].

That idea inspired many of the people who went to Seattle. The churches were there, many concerned about world poverty; there were environmentalists, animal-welfare groups, trade unionists and those who campaign for the cancellation of Third World debt. All were immediately denounced as anarchists, extremists, members of the mob, and so on. The police in Seattle put up a pretty good show of organising a Tiananmen Square operation without the killings. When I saw the police in their *Star Wars* outfits and the arrest of 500 people who wanted only justice for their own people, it gave me an indication of what it is all about.

The Internet plays a very important part in these matters because, through it, all the groups sent out their messages. They could not get their messages across through Rupert Murdoch, CNN or the BBC, but they could communicate directly. They have no leaders to be demonised by the press; groups turned up with their own faith.

In the next century, people want cooperation and not competition in self-sustaining economies, working with other nations. They want security in their lives – and that does not mean more nuclear weapons. They want to plan for peace as we have always planned for war, with a single-minded determination to meet our needs. They want democratic control over their own destiny. That is the real lesson that this century must teach the next one.

I shall finish with a quote that, in a way, sums up what I feel on this issue:

> We have lived so long at the mercy of uncontrolled economic forces that we have become sceptical about any plan for human emancipation. Such a rational and deliberate reorganisation of our economic life would enable us, out of the increased wealth production, to establish an irreducible minimum standard which might progressively be raised to one of comfort and security.

Those are the words of Harold Macmillan in his book *The Middle Way*. I sat in Parliament with that man – the great-grandfather of the Wets, who was well to the left of the present government.

If as a democrat, an internationalist and a committed socialist I may endorse that view, I suspect that I would be doing so with the support of most people in the world, who do not benefit from the worship of money that we have been celebrating in this strange religious festival that we call a debate.

6

Justice

*The problems facing single parents, who were to be denied a portion
of their income by the new Labour government, and the denial of the
right of women to be ordained in the Church of England, formed the
subject of speeches made in 1997 and 1993 in the Commons. I am
particularly pleased that the ordination of women was finally agreed
upon by the Church, because it was a cause to which both my
parents were strongly committed.*

HOUSE OF COMMONS DEBATE ON THE SOCIAL SECURITY
BILL, 10 DECEMBER 1997

I joined a Parliament in 1950 that had taken over a Britain that
was battered, bombed and bankrupt. That Parliament's first action
was to treble the widow's pension from ten shillings a week to
twenty-six shillings a week. That bankrupt nation introduced a
free health service, and did not have much of a problem with the

welfare bill when unemployment was so low, because we were building houses and hospitals and recruiting teachers and nurses.

I was a minister in subsequent Labour governments that brought pensions into line with earnings. I am very proud of that. As Secretary of State for Energy, I also introduced a scheme to ensure that everyone on benefit had a 25 per cent cut in their winter fuel bills, regardless of the temperature. All that is dismissed as old Labour, but I am very proud of it. The arguments for the bill, which have been well rehearsed, run counter to the beliefs that I have and that the Labour Party had – the beliefs that brought me into Parliament and led me to join the Labour Party on my seventeenth birthday in 1942.

I must say, very respectfully, that the government have not taken a hard decision; they have taken the easiest decision possible, hammering the poorest people who have no bargaining power. They have ring-fenced the richest people, promising them that there will be no increase in income tax. Anyone who has had experience of single parents – up to a couple of thousand have been to my surgeries over the years – knows that the children of split families are affected by their circumstances. They want their mother or father close to them when the other partner leaves. We are going back to the Victorian concept of the deserving poor, who want work, and the undeserving poor, who prefer to look after their children.

I am opposed to the philosophy of the bill. Every argument that I have heard from the Front Bench has convinced me more and more that this is a bad measure . . .

I have found today's debate fascinating, because politics has come back to the Chamber of the House of Commons. Some of us, including me – I make nothing of that – want hon. Members to say the same in opposition and in government. We want some attempt to be made to assess the rights and wrongs of matters, rather than decisions being taken on the basis of an economic analysis founded on some requirement to be competitive and productive. The cuts that the Cabinet made twenty-one years ago cost us the 1979 election. Denis Healey, who is an honest man, has admitted that those cuts were unnecessary.

I do not ask anyone else who has not had my experiences to follow me into the Lobby if there is a vote, but I shall vote against the bill, because this is what Parliament is about. If we separate this place from the concerns outside, there will be a price not just for the party of which I am proud to be a member, but for the reputation of the parliamentary process, as people become more and more despairing because their concerns are not being listened to.

HOUSE OF COMMONS DEBATE ON THE ORDINATION OF WOMEN IN THE CHURCH OF ENGLAND, 29 OCTOBER 1993

Conscience is not the exclusive property of men. Many women moved to service in the Church have waited most patiently, not for five years but for seventy or more.

During the last world war, the Bishop of Chekiang ordained Miss Lee Timoi to give Holy Communion in that province of China. At the end of the war, the Church of England said to the Bishop, 'If you do not remove her orders to prevent her from giving Holy Communion, we will stop giving money to the Church of China.'

We are discussing human matters because matters of faith are deeply entrenched in the human soul. I had more happiness from seeing the young women outside Church House embracing each other when the news of the vote in the Synod [approving the

ordination of women] came through than I have had from many
of the decisions taken by this House over many years. Women
have waited patiently for ordination. I have met – as I am sure
others have – young women training for ordination, yet without
any knowledge of when they would ever be ordained in the Church
of England.

The arguments used by the right hon. Member for Suffolk,
Coastal [John Gummer] – who, dare I say, has no theological qualifications – to persuade Parliament to turn down the Measure were
absolutely invalid. As the Second Church Estates Commissioner,
the right hon. Member for Selby [Michael Alison] said, the
Anglican communion worldwide has already accepted the ordination of women. Bishop Harris – a woman – is an Episcopalian
bishop in America and she may come to the next Lambeth conference. Is that a breach of the unity on which we are so often
lectured? A year or two ago, I met an American woman who had
been ordained into the Episcopalian Church and she gave
Communion in this country. That is one reason why I ask what
offence would be committed. When she gave Communion, an
Anglican vicar approached the Communion table and bit her on
the thumb when she administered the Sacrament to him.

We must recognise that at the heart of this debate, however it
may be covered up in theological terms, is prejudice against women
and the attitude that they are not human beings. The right hon.
Member for Suffolk, Coastal, says that the great thing about the
Church of England is that it is comprehensive. What is the price
of being comprehensive if the Church will not give women the
opportunity to serve it through ordination?

As I have said, matters of faith are deeply felt. I have a great
respect for people of all faiths. So few people believe in anything

Name BENN
Anthony Neil Wedgwood
Description Pilot Officer

Unit Royal Airforce

From left: me as a Private, Home Guard 1942; a Pilot Officer, RAF 1945; and a Sub-Lieutenant, Fleet Air Arm, 1945.

Page 3.
Navy Form S.1511
**NAVAL
IDENTITY CARD No.** 185

EUT: [A]

Signature of Bearer A. N. W. Benn
Visible distinguishing marks
CAR ON LEFT WRIST

(*Left*) Flying solo in a Fairchild Cornell, Rhodesia, 1944.
(*Middle*) Formation flying an Airspeed Oxford, Rhodesia, 1944. (*Right*) On 'Wings' parade, Rhodesia, March 8, 1945.

(Right) My first meeting with Caroline (2 August, 1948): Tony Crosland offered to photograph a re-staging of the moment, a year later in 1949.

(Left) Sitting on the bench on which I proposed to Caroline in 1948 at Oxford; an event also photographed by Tony Crosland a year later.

Caroline with Tony Crosland, back from the 'Paras' and by 1949 a don at Trinity College, Oxford.

Mr and Mrs Benn-to-be
at Stansgate, 1948, before
Caroline returned to Cincinnati.

Caroline with our first car,
a Morris Oxford, which lasted
from 1928 to 1954. Its successor,
another Morris Oxford, is still
at Stansgate.

(*Left*) Caroline at her home, on the morning of our wedding, 17 June, 1949.
(*Right*) And, a few hours later, at the Church of the Advent in Cincinnati.

A beautiful bride.

Nurse Olive Winch (Buddy) with my first son, Stephen, July 1952.

Cincinnati, 1959, with Caroline's parents (seated, below me), her brother Graydon (to left), and Caroline's sister, Nance (to right). Our four children are seated among the grown-ups.

Sitting on our special bench, 1979

In Loving Memory of
Caroline Middleton DeCamp Benn
Author   Teacher   Socialist
Born Cincinnati   13 October 1926
Died London   22 November 2000

Caroline's gravestone at Stansgate (bust by Ian Walters)

Speaker Martin conferring the 'Freedom of the House' at my retirement party, May 2001. Cake designed and commissioned by Ruth Winstone.

Benn family photo, Christmas 2003

today that when we meet people of conviction, of any sort, we must respect them. The hon. Member for Maidstone [Ann Widdecombe] has, I believe, left the Church of England. Of course, it is a fact that in America many Roman Catholics joined the Episcopalian Church when it ordained women. The hon. Lady must not rule out the possibility that, as a result of the ordination of women, Roman Catholic women will join the Church of England so that they, too, can be ordained . . .

I am not making any theological argument, because I do not pretend to believe in anything more than the priesthood of all believers. I have never believed in bishops, any more than I believe in regional organisers. All organisations in the world begin with a burning faith and end up with a bureaucracy more interested in burning and expelling people than in the faith that brought them into being. I will not go into that in any greater detail.

Should Parliament decide this matter? Of course, in law it must, because the Church of England is a nationalised Church. It is our oldest nationalised industry. The right hon. Member for Suffolk, Coastal, said that Henry VIII nationalised it so that it could be a Church of the people. In fact, he nationalised it because he had a row with the Pope, who was imposing too much taxation on Britain. The King wanted the tax instead of the Pope. It was what one might call a value-added tax argument in theological terms.

Do not let us be told that it was because, in the Tudor settlement, the King suddenly was moved to provide spiritual comfort. There is not a word of truth in that.

The Act of Uniformity has been very brutal in its implications. A Revd William Benn – I do not know whether he was an ancestor, but I hope to God that he was – was ejected from his living in Dorchester in 1662 under the Great Ejectment because he would not accept the provisions of the Act of Uniformity. Everyone knows that the Church has been most intolerant as a nationalised Church. At one time, Catholics and Jews could not sit in the House. Everyone must know the story of Charles Bradlaugh who was elected to represent Northampton. He said, 'I cannot take the oath because I am a Humanist.' The House said, 'Sling him out.' There was another election and he was returned again, and the same thing happened. On the third occasion – being a reasonable, moderate man – Bradlaugh said, 'All right, I will take the oath.' The House told him, 'You can't, because you are not a Christian.' At that point, the Speaker intervened with the sort of discretion that only Speakers have and said, 'I instruct the hon. Gentleman to take the oath.' The Church of England should not be presented historically as anything other than it was – a state Church which was sometimes enormously intolerant, but which has gradually come to recognise that there are other views as well.

Has any right hon. or hon. Member read the homage that a bishop must recite before he is ordained? It reads:

I do hereby declare that your Majesty is the only supreme governor of this your Realm in spiritual and ecclesiastical things as well as in temporal

– bishops do not even recognise democracy –

and that no foreign prelate or potentate has any jurisdiction within this Realm.

The Maastricht Treaty will be ratified today, yet every bishop has taken an oath that 'no foreign prelate or potentate has any jurisdiction within this Realm'.

Let us be clear. If the Queen became a Catholic this afternoon, the throne would be vacated. Something else will happen – she will become a citizen of the European Union. Perhaps she could go to the European Court and say, 'I have lost my job because I have changed my religion.' Let us be sensible. It is time to be rid of all that.

I heard that the Queen had to give her consent to the Measure – and I know that because I have often sought her consent to establish a republic and to other minor measures of that kind – before we could discuss the ordination of women, yet she is supposed to be the supreme spiritual governor of the Church. What are the Prince of Wales's theological qualifications in this matter passes beyond belief, but he owns some benefices in Cornwall, so he had to consent, too.

A couple of days ago, the judges intervened with a judicial review of the ordination of women. On Monday, I wrote an angry letter to the Speaker because I thought that the arrogance of the judges had gone beyond control. I was reassured by the Clerk that the judges did what they ought to have done. What nonsense that is.

There is no spiritual requirement for being a Member of Parliament. I should be surprised if any right hon. or hon. Member put in his last election address, 'If elected, I will vote against the ordination of women' or mentioned the matter in any speech. No one has the political mandate, spiritual authority or denominational requirement to do that.

As to the House of Lords deciding the matter, the last ten Prime

Ministers put 800 people in another place. Are those party placemen to judge whether women are qualified to become ordained? That is an impossible position.

I believe that the Church of England will free itself before the end of this century, and I hope that it does so by agreement. If we turn down this Measure, then, candidly, I believe that it will accelerate disestablishment because the Church will not have it – rightly so. But I do not want the freedom of the Church of England to come as a result of a row, but by general agreement.

There is one other matter that I find offensive. I know that the Church Estates Commissioner has a job to do, but I found it offensive to be told that the House need not worry because there will be safeguards for male priests against ordained women coming into their parishes. Safeguards? My God – what sort of man wants a safeguard in case a woman gives Communion in his parish?

I will vote for the Measure because I do not believe that we have any right in the matter. As to offering safeguards and financial compensation, if it is a matter of conscience, how many people have gone to the stake for exercising their consciences? Would Cranmer have withdrawn if the Church had offered him a cheque? Are we to believe that in a deeply spiritual matter, conscience can be overcome with money? Are we to believe that a chaplain in a private school that requires an Anglican cannot carry on because of the thought that a woman might approach his school with the Sacrament, and that money would settle his conscientious objection? The House is facing an absurdity.

If any compensation is to be given, it should be given to the women who have waited so patiently for the right to be ordained and to be called to serve. Compensation for the promotion of women is not an unattractive idea. When Mrs Thatcher became

Prime Minister, we might all have been compensated for the awful business of seeing her exercise supreme power. When my right hon. Friend the Member for Derby, South [Margaret Beckett] was made deputy leader of my party, I would have been happy – having once aspired to that post – to receive some beneficial bounty from Walworth Road. Even when the Labour Party ceased to be a socialist party, I did not ask for compensation. I do not see why Church of England vicars should obtain it.

I hope that I have not detained the House or diverted it from a very important decision. I hope to live to see the day when a woman Archbishop of Canterbury greets a Pope in a Church that has ordained women. If that sounds a little extreme, it is no more extreme than a Member of Parliament telling a male-dominated House of Commons ninety years ago that one day a woman Speaker would preside over its proceedings.

7

Democracy

My commitment to parliamentary democracy grew inevitably out of my family's roots in Parliament, and has been strengthened by witnessing the abuse of power. The right to know, the right to vote and the right to decide are crucial for a society that claims to be self-governing. Yet each generation has to reassert these demands, which are easily denied and threatened by the powerful.

HOUSE OF COMMONS DEBATE ON THE ELECTION OF BETTY BOOTHROYD AS SPEAKER, 27 APRIL 1992

This debate was chaired by Edward Heath as Father of the House; the Speakership was contested, rather than given to a senior member of either the Labour or Conservative Party, and Members of Parliament chose Betty Boothroyd, the first woman to hold the post.

You, Sir Edward, and I have sat in thirteen Parliaments under seven Speakers, and I think that we are the last remaining

Members of the House who saw Attlee and Churchill at the Dispatch Box and heard the last King's Speech from the throne. We were elected in the same year; you are the Father of the House and I was then the baby of the House. I must now be the uncle of the House, and it is in that capacity that I want to speak. My hon. Friend the Member for Linlithgow [Tam Dalyell] introduced, in my opinion, the most important element into this debate – the Speakership itself. As a young Member I once moved a motion of censure on the Speaker – a daring thing to do, for which I paid a heavy price. I did it because he refused me an emergency debate on the possibility of military action in Oman. Also, I was kept out by Harry Hylton-Foster on the ground that I was a peer, so I have had conflicts with one or two other Speakers as well.

Before we come to the names – there is a candidate whom I strongly wish to support – I wish to stress that this is a House of Commons matter. Previously, Speakers have been chosen by patronage, nudging and winks, through the usual channels, which are the most polluted waterways in the world. All the candidates who have been mentioned have exceptional qualities – I am not arguing about that – but the House should remember that the reason that we regard the Speaker as important is that in this Chamber – or where it was 450 years ago this year – Mr Speaker Lenthall refused to bow to the King when he wanted to arrest five Members. He said, using the famous phrase, 'May it please Your Majesty, I have neither eyes to see, nor Tongue to Speak in this Place, but as the House is pleased to direct me, whose servant I am here.'

Therefore, if we are talking about the Speakership, we must bring it up to date and ask where executive power lies now and how the House can be strong in defending it. We need a Speaker who will defend the legislature against the Executive, and defend the electors against those who abuse power, whether it be state power or private power.

The power of Charles I has long gone and his successors have no power left, but in that 450 years state power has grown enormously in many ways. For example – and I am looking at the Prime Minister [John Major] – all the prerogatives that Charles had are now in the Prime Minister's hands. You, Sir Edward, know it yourself. The Prime Minister can take the country to war without consulting Parliament – he did. He can sign treaties and choose archbishops without consulting Parliament. He can create peers without consulting Parliament – the previous ten Prime Ministers have created 800 Members of the other place without doing so. The Prime Minister can, without consulting Parliament, agree to laws being made in secret in the Council of Ministers in Brussels that take precedence over our laws. He also has other powers. Therefore, the divine right of kings is alive and well in the person of the Prime Minister of the day.

Other powers have grown: the City of London votes every day, and so will the European Central Bank, to decide the policy of this government and every other government. We are no longer even the primary source of debate, as television has taken it over. Mr Speaker Sissons and Mr Speaker Paxman presumed to tell us what the nation should think. When I first came here the Division Lobbies and polling stations were supposed to be the places where the nation's will was expressed, but now the arrogant pollsters – the inaccurate pollsters – presume to tell us what the nation thinks. I say to whoever succeeds to the Chair that democracy is being bypassed, and the responsibility for that rests largely with the House of Commons and all the parties which have allowed it to happen.

We have some powers: we can speak freely. Our speeches are printed in Hansard – the only newspaper not owned by Rupert Murdoch. We also have access to television, without being interrogated in the star chamber by David Dimbleby. But our most powerful weapon is Mr Speaker, and I wish to speak about the Speakership.

Apart from keeping order, which is not as difficult as it might appear, the Speaker can allow or disallow parliamentary questions to ministers, and thus expose or protect them; accept or refuse closure motions, which can prolong or stop debates; select or reject Back-Bench motions or amendments, and thus deny a minority view in the House from ever being put in the Lobbies; permit or deny private notice questions or emergency debates; call or not call individual Members; and give or withhold precedence to Privy Counsellors, which is the source of much anger. He can determine which Bills are hybrid and which are not; use a casting vote if there is a tie; recall the Commons in a recess – a formidable power – in the event of some international crisis; certify a money Bill; and rule on matters of privilege.

That is the office which we are discussing and, although the vote will resolve who occupies the Chair, we must pay attention to the office itself. Every Member present brings his or her own experience and convictions to the House. We were not elected to be robots, trembling before the party Whips. Ultimately, we are responsible to ourselves and our consciences. All party leaders get it wrong sometimes and, often, one lone voice may turn out to have got it right. We must speak out more plainly for the people we represent, many of whom have no confidence in the House. The hon. Member for Orkney and Shetland [James Wallace] questioned whether this is a representative assembly. That is now on the agenda, whether we agree or not. Ethnic communities and those who poured into the polling stations but could not vote because they did not pay their poll tax do not feel represented in the House. Others can live abroad for twenty-five years and still have a vote without even being asked to pay poll tax.

The point is that we must not have another cosy little election for a Speaker without recognising that these are difficult times. I believe – I have been here for a long time – that we need a reforming Speaker. We modernise everything, but the Speakership goes on. We need a Speaker to call more Members from minority parties and more minority Members from other parties. We need more debates on emergency matters – why should the television channels cover matters that we cannot discuss even when the business of the House is only a trifling amendment on a government Bill? I want a Speaker who will demand better conditions for the staff who work in the Palace of Westminster, including comprehensive and complete childcare for the many parents who have come to the House: I should like a Speaker who will allow Westminster Hall to be used so that we do not leave pensioners freezing outside in the winter when they come to lobby their Members of Parliament. I should like the Strangers Gallery to be renamed the 'Electors Gallery'. We have never caught up with 1832 when this place was done out.

I should also like a Speaker who does not wear a wig every day, because it is so intimidating – [Interruption.] I know that Mr Speaker Weatherill was popular on television, but many people watching thought that he was appearing in the High Court. We need a Speaker who will defend the rights of those represented here.

Although I am not speaking for my hon. Friend the Member for West Bromwich, West [Betty Boothroyd], whom I support, I hope that she and the other candidates are listening. If Parliament is to survive, it must be a workshop, not a museum. For one reason or another, the years ahead will be very troubled. There will not only be difficulties in the House, but social unrest – [*Interruption.*] I am giving my opinion to the House – I thought that that was what the House was famous for. I do not believe that democracy can be taken for granted anywhere. We would do well to elect a Speaker who will help to do the difficult task that falls to those of us who have the honour to serve in this House.

HOUSE OF COMMONS DEBATE ON PARLIAMENTARY DEMOCRACY, 13 MAY 1999

. . . I hope that the Hansard of today's debate is not made available to our troops and airmen involved in the war in Kosovo. Most hon. Members know that, over recent years and for a variety of reasons, Parliament has become less and less relevant to decision-making in our society. To avoid following the pattern of the previous speakers, I should point out that the process of by-passing Parliament; the centralisation of power; the use of patronage; and the use of the royal prerogative to avoid serious debate began under earlier governments and is being continued under the present government.

I wish to speak about the relevance of this debate to next Tuesday's debate on Kosovo. My hon. Friend the Member for Linlithgow [Tam Dalyell] and I have asked on a number of occasions – the request has been echoed by Opposition Members –

for the House of Commons to be allowed to express its view on this major war, which is involving not only our servicemen but their families, and which will cost the people of this country a great deal. The government have consistently refused to allow that.

I asked my right hon. Friend the Leader of the House [Margaret Beckett] – whom I have known and worked with closely over the years – whether we could have a vote. In reply, on 22 April, she said, Although I well understand the express wish of Members on both sides of the House for a decision-making procedure of the type that he describes and suggests, there is no precedent for that in the House [*Official Report*, 22 April 1999; vol. 329, c. 1053].

That is to say that the present government, who are committed to modernisation, are basing their decisions on the medieval principle that the question of going to war is a matter of royal prerogative – and so indeed it is.

I looked back to the journals of the House for 1621 – a month or two before I got here – when James I sent a direction to the House of Commons that it had no business discussing foreign or defence policy. The House passed a protestation, and the King then dissolved Parliament. The question whether the legislature has any role in the conduct of foreign and defence policy must concern people who take different views in this House.

Some of my hon. Friends are in favour of the deployment of ground troops and of stepping up the bombing, and should be allowed to express that view in the Lobby. Others, such as myself, think that the venture was ill judged, ill thought out and has failed. I should be allowed to express that view, on behalf of the people who elected me. A vote could then take place. If we are to discuss parliamentary democracy – as distinct from this debate between the Conservative and Liberal Democrat parties, which may have been fun for them but was not for me – we ought to discuss that matter.

For our children, we describe ourselves as a democracy. I always attend state occasions and, in this House, we talk about a parliamentary democracy. When the Queen makes a speech, she does not mention either word – she says that we are a constitutional monarchy. There is all the difference in the world between a democracy, a parliamentary democracy and a constitutional monarchy . . . When we meet, I have to tell a lie to sit in this House – I must say: 'I swear by almighty God that I will bear faithful and true allegiance.'

I do not believe that – I am a republican. Every minister must swear an oath of allegiance. The Privy Counsellors' oath is even worse. They must say that they will defend the monarch from 'foreign prelates, potentates and powers'. When they go as Commissioners to Brussels, Privy Counsellors take another oath, and say that they will take no notice of any nation that might put pressure upon them. These may not seem to be significant questions, but they become so when a war occurs and we are not consulted.

I wish to refer to the growth in patronage. All Prime Ministers appoint all the bishops; why cannot the Church of England have the confidence to choose its own leaders? Why cannot we select or vet judges in the way that the Senate does in the United States? The Prime Minister has just appointed a new Commissioner to Brussels who, I understand, is not even the choice of the Conservative Party. He has used his patronage to appoint a

Conservative representing a different view, but that is the practice. All ministers are appointed and dismissed by the Prime Minister.

If the Labour evidence given to the royal commission on the reform of the House of Lords is to be believed, all the House of Lords is to be appointed. Some wonder whether it is not the intention to appoint the whole House of Commons, but we have not reached that stage yet. It is certainly true that the use of party patronage in choosing a First Minister in Wales or a mayor in London, or disposing of my hon. Friend the Member for Falkirk, West [Dennis Canavan], shows a desire to control everything.

Everyone with power wants to do that, so we must ask not why they do it, but why we accept it. The House has the capacity to do something about it. I introduced the Crown Prerogatives (Parliamentary Control) Bill.

The Crown Prerogatives (Parliamentary Control) Bill was supported by my hon. Friends the Members for Linlithgow, for Preston [Audrey Wise] and for Nottingham, South [Alan Simpson]; by my hon. and learned Friend the Member for Medway [Robert Marshall-Andrews]; by my right hon. Friend the Member for Bishop Auckland [Derek Foster]; by the hon. Members for Lewes [Norman Baker], for North Antrim [Revd Ian Paisley], for Aldridge-Brownhills [Richard Shepherd] and for Billericay [Teresa Gorman]; and by the right hon. Members for Haltemprice and Howden [David Davis] and for Caernarfon [Dafydd Wigley]. That is broad support. Even the former Prime Minister, the right hon. Member for Huntingdon [John Major] signed an early-day motion calling for the Commissioners to be approved by the House of Commons.

Trying to be constructive, I consulted the seventeenth-century precedents, when the abuse of Executive power had reached similar proportions, and decided that we should send a humble address to Her Majesty. I have drafted it, and I would be grateful for support from all parties. I have written to certain Privy Counsellors.

The draft reads:

> That a Humble Address be presented to Her Majesty praying that the Royal Prerogatives relating to the making of war and the commitment of the Armed Services to the present military operations in the Balkans be now placed at the disposal of the House of Commons for the purpose of permitting Members of Parliament to debate and vote upon a substantive Motion on the merits of that policy and any alternative Motions that might be moved designed to lay the foundations of a just and peaceful settlement in line with Britain's international obligations.

I wish that this debate was about our role. The media have taken over. The governor of a Central Bank, not elected by proportional representation, although one might have expected that from those who favour it, is coming along, as is Rupert Murdoch. They are squeezing us . . .

We must restore parliamentary democracy in Britain before it is ultimately squeezed out. I genuinely fear that, so I hope that the speeches that follow will not be a further exchange of hustings schoolboy abuse, but will try seriously to address the question that must concern us all: have the House of Commons and the people whom we represent any role whatever in the decisions that matter in our lives, or are we merely spectators of our fate, and not participants in the future that we want to shape?

HOUSE OF COMMONS SPEECH DURING THE PASSAGE OF THE FREEDOM OF INFORMATION BILL, 5 APRIL 2000

First, I congratulate the Members of the House on both sides who have fought this campaign. I regard this as the beginning of a recovery of power by the legislature in dealing with the Executive. This debate and its conclusion will be seen as very significant in the development of parliamentary democracy.

Of course, there have been some moves towards this. The government of whom I was a Member introduced Green Papers to allow consultation. However, the Bill is a disappointment. The older I get, the more I realise how difficult past reforms were. I am not sure that the Home Secretary [Jack Straw] would encourage the publication of Hansard. He might well say – [*Interruption*] Hon. Members laugh, but there was a battle; Hansard was put in prison. I am not joking. The argument would be that it would not be in the public interest for the public to know what was said in Parliament.

We are approaching the heart of the democratic deficit. Ministers say, 'The democratic deficit means that I must decide, not the House of Commons.' However, the fault line in democracy does not lie in what ministers say. When we first arrive at the House as MPs, we all have to take an oath of allegiance to the Crown. As this is the High Court of Parliament, I always assumed that I should take an oath to tell the truth, the whole truth and nothing but the truth. That seems to be an appropriate oath for a Member approaching the High Court of Parliament. Privy Counsellors take another oath. The truth is that, at that moment, the Executive, in the form of ministers, are standing against Parliament and the public interest. That is what the matter is really about.

Ministers are often kept in the dark. When I was in the Cabinet, I once said that I wished we had freedom of information for Cabinet ministers – but that was seen as an inappropriate joke. However, I should be very surprised if the Home Secretary knows much about what the security services are doing. If he does, he is the first Home Secretary ever to do so. He is a manager and we are representatives. The division between the government and the House is the real division.

The longer I served in government – I was a minister for eleven years – the more I found that it was easy for people to confuse the public interest with the convenience of ministers. That is easy to do; if it embarrasses ministers, it cannot be in the public interest – but in fact, it is not in the interest of ministers.

That argument leads to another point: I cannot think of any secrets that I ever knew. I do not want to disappoint those Members who are hoping for office, but those of us who have held office know that there are few secrets in government. I knew what would be in the Budget twenty-four hours before it was announced, and was afraid that I should sleepwalk and tell somebody. I knew that we were going to devalue the pound forty-eight hours before we did so. I knew the government's position on negotiations with foreign governments – that all came out when the negotiations took place. I knew what would be in the honours list before it came out – but everybody knows that.

In the old days, if the fact that a man was to be given a peerage was leaked, that ruled it out completely. Nowadays, the immigration laws have been amended; if one agrees to live here, one is put in the House of Lords. However, that is another question.

The real reason why I want to contribute to the debate is because of the nuclear industry, for which I had responsibility for many years. Recent events at Sellafield confirm what I learned by experience; even as a minister – let alone a Member of Parliament – I was never told the truth by the nuclear industry. For example, I found out about the fire at Windscale – now called Sellafield – only when I visited Tokyo. My officials had never told me about it. When I asked them why they had not done so, they said, 'It was before you were a minister.'

When the Americans discovered that there had been an explosion at Khysthm, the major Soviet reprocessing plant, I was never told. I asked the Chairman of the Atomic Energy Authority, 'Why didn't you tell me?' He replied, 'We were told by the Central Intelligence Agency not to tell British ministers, because it could create concern about the safety of nuclear power.'

It was not until I left office that I discovered that, while I had been making honest speeches about atoms for peace, all the plutonium from our civil nuclear power stations was going to America to make the bomb. The atoms-for-peace power stations were bomb factories for the Pentagon. I felt affronted by that. Had people known the facts at the time, the development of the debate on nuclear power and the nuclear industry would have been much better informed. We should not have had the problem at Sellafield, because the matter would probably have been dealt with earlier.

These provisions are probably the most important in the Bill. After thirty years, we can find out at the Public Record Office what ministers have done, but if we want the public to have an influence on their government, they must know about the debate before it is concluded. I realise that there are arguments about fact and advice, but I have never believed that information about the nature of government policy-making was damaging.

What is damaging are leaks, malice, and so on . . . People with knowledge of a situation could contribute. The trouble with the official secrets that surround the government is that they lock ministers in with their officials.

Some ministers are rather like constitutional monarchs. They can say yes or no to their Permanent Secretaries. However, once we let it be known publicly that we are considering a matter, we make available to ministers a range of advice that they would not be able to get from within Whitehall, and that allows them to become umpires between their civil servants and public expertise outside. I therefore make the case – I hope that it does not shock anyone – that open government and freedom of information are good for ministers, not just for Parliament and the public. That argument needs examination . . .

I hope that public opinion makes it clear to the Home Secretary and others that we are not prepared to accept that we should be treated as children and left outside the inner knowledge of what happens. It denies ministers the advice that they need, and the public the opportunity to participate in some way in their future, rather than being just spectators of their fate.

HOUSE OF COMMONS DEBATE ON THE EUROPEAN COMMUNITY, 20 NOVEMBER 1991

Prime Minister John Major took part in crucial meetings (inter-governmental conferences) in late 1991, meetings that were to result in Britain's agreement to the Treaty on European Union (the Maastricht Treaty) of December 1991. This established the European Union in place of the Community, and expanded political, economic and social integration among the member states.

Three points about the debate have interested me. First, there is fundamental agreement among the three party leaders. The Prime Minister is on the eve of negotiations so he has to be cautious. The Leader of the Opposition [Neil Kinnock], who hopes to take over, can be bolder. The Liberal Democrats, who are far from office, can be quite clear about their objective. There is no disagreement about the idea, that we should move from the original membership of the Community through the Single European Act to something stronger. Secondly, a degree of caution has emerged from people who, when they discussed the matter twenty years ago, were far more uncritical. Thirdly – I say this with some satisfaction – twenty-one years after I urged a referendum, I have won the right hon. Member for Finchley [Margaret Thatcher] and the right hon. Member for Yeovil [Paddy Ashdown] to my cause. I had to wait twenty-one years, but it has been worth waiting for some recognition of the fact that the people have a right to a say in their government.

I do not want to go over old ground, because this is not a question of yes or no to the status quo; we are looking to the future. Some people genuinely believe that we shall never get social justice from the British government, but we shall get it from Jacques Delors. They believe that a good king is better than a bad Parliament. I have never taken that view. Others believe that the change is inevitable, and that the common currency will protect us from inflation and will provide a wage policy. They believe that it will control speculation and that Britain cannot survive alone. None of those arguments persuade me because the argument has never been about sovereignty.

I do not know what a sovereign is, apart from the one that used to be in gold, and the Pope, who is a sovereign in the Vatican. We are talking about democracy. No nation – not even the great

United States which could, for all I know, be destroyed by a nuclear weapon from a Third World country – has the power to impose its will on other countries. We are discussing whether the British people are to be allowed to elect those who make the laws under which they are governed. The argument is nothing to do with whether we should get more maternity leave from Madame Papandreou than from Madame Thatcher. That is not the issue.

I recognise that, when the members of the three Front Benches agree, I am in a minority. My next job therefore is to explain to the people of Chesterfield what we have decided. I will say first, 'My dear constituents, in future you will be governed by people whom you do not elect and cannot remove. I am sorry about it. They may give you better crèches and shorter working hours but you cannot remove them.'

I know that it sounds negative, but I have always thought it positive to say that the important thing about democracy is that we can remove without bloodshed the people who govern us. We can get rid of a Callaghan, a Wilson or even a right hon. Lady by internal processes. We can get rid of the right hon. Member for Huntingdon [John Major]. But that cannot be done in the structure that is proposed. Even if one likes the policies of the people in Europe, one cannot get rid of them . . .

We must ask what will happen when people realise what we have done. We have had a marvellous debate about Europe, but none of us has discussed our relationship with the people who sent us here. Hon. Members have expressed views on Albania and the Baltic States. I have been dazzled by the knowledge of the continent of which we are all part. No one has spoken about how he or she got here and what we were sent here to do.

If people lose the power to sack their government, one of several things happens. First, people may just slope off. Apathy could destroy democracy. When the turnout drops below 50 per cent, we are in danger . . .

The second thing that people can do is to riot. Riot is an old-fashioned method of drawing the attention of the government to what is wrong. It is difficult for an elected person to admit it, but the riot at Strangeways produced some prison reforms. Riot has historically played a much larger part in British politics than we are ever allowed to know.

Thirdly, nationalism can arise. Instead of blaming the Treaty of Rome, people say, 'It is those Germans', or, 'It is the French.' Nationalism is built out of frustration that people feel when they cannot get their way through the ballot box. With nationalism comes repression. I hope that it is not pessimistic – in my view it is not – to say that democracy hangs by a thread in every country of the world. Unless we can offer people a peaceful route to the resolution of injustices through the ballot box, they will not listen to a House that has blocked off that route. There are many alternatives open to us . . . this is not the only Europe on offer.

I understand that my hon. Friend the Member for Sunderland, South [Chris Mullin], is a democratic federalist, as is my hon. Friend the Member for Derbyshire, North-East [Harry Barnes]. They want an American-type constitution for Europe. It could be that our laws would hang on which way the Albanian members voted. I could not complain about that, because that is democracy, but it is unworkable. It is like trying to get an elephant to dance through a minefield, but it would be democratic.

Another way would be to have a looser, wider Europe. I have an idea for a Commonwealth of Europe. I am introducing a Bill on the subject. Europe would be rather like the British

Commonwealth. We would work by consent with people. Or we could accept this ghastly proposal, which is clumsy, secretive, centralised, bureaucratic and divisive. That is how I regard the Treaty of Rome. I was born a European and I will die one, but I have never put my alliance behind the Treaty of Rome. I object to it. I hate being called an anti-European. How can one be anti-European when one is born in Europe? It is like saying that one is anti-British if one does not agree with the Chancellor of the Exchequer. What a lot of nonsense it is.

If democracy is destroyed in Britain, it will be not the communists, Trotskyists or subversives, but this House which threw it away. The rights that are entrusted to us are not for us to give away. Even if I agree with everything that is proposed, I cannot hand away powers lent to me for five years by the people of Chesterfield. I just could not do it. It would be theft of public rights.

My last parliamentary speech, 22 March 2001

This speech was made following the report of the Procedure Select Committee, which proposed changes to the way the Speaker is elected by the House of Commons.

I ask the indulgence of the House. This may be my last speech, so if I am out of order, Mr Speaker, I hope that you will allow me to range widely.

I support the report of the Procedure Committee and the motion proposed by my right hon. Friend the Leader of the House [Margaret Beckett]. The report is scholarly and historical; it considers all the arguments. My only difference with it is over the question of a secret ballot. I have always understood that if one votes as oneself, it must be secret. Years ago, when I was canvassing in Bristol, I asked a woman to support me and she replied, 'Mr Benn, the ballet is secret.' I thought of her dancing alone in the bedroom, where no candidate was allowed to know about it. However, when we vote in a representative capacity, people must know what we have done, so I shall vote for the amendment. The Committee has done very well. I hope that the House accepts the report.

The old system had serious difficulties. Although I disagreed strongly with the Father of the House [Edward Heath], he carried out his duties with exceptional skill – with panache! I felt that he was the only Member of the House who could have turned the Beefeaters into a fighting force – he showed such passion and commitment to the rules. We got the Speaker we wanted and I hope that, as a result of today's proceedings, we shall get the system we want – the one that I advocated, as the House will recall.

As I have done on previous occasions – when we were electing a Speaker – I want to look a little more broadly at the role of the Speaker. Often, we tend to think of the Speaker in relation only to the Chamber, but the Speaker's role is of much wider importance. Relations between the legislature and the Executive go through the Speaker of the House.

We live in a strange country: we do not elect our head of state; we do not elect the second Chamber. We elect only this House, and even in this House enormous power is vested in the prerogatives. The Prime Minister can go to war without consulting us, sign treaties without consulting us, agree to laws in Brussels without consulting us, and appoint bishops, peers and judges without consulting us. The role of the Speaker today compared with that of Mr Speaker Lenthall is that you, Mr Speaker, are protecting us from the triple powers of Buckingham Palace, the Millbank Tower and Central Office, which, in combination, represent as serious a challenge to our role.

Then there is the link between the Commons and the people. I have seen many schoolchildren taken around the House, and have talked to some of them about how it has been a home of democracy for hundreds of years. In 1832, only 2 per cent of the population had the vote. That may seem a long time ago, but it was only eighteen years before my grandfather was born. When I was born, women were not allowed the vote until they were thirty. Democracy – input from the people – is very, very new. The link between popular consent and the decisions of the House can be tenuous.

Furthermore, nowadays, Parliament representing the will of the people has to cope with many extra-parliamentary forces – very threatening extra-parliamentary forces. I refer not to demonstrations, but to the power of the media, the power of the multinationals, the power of Brussels and the power of the World Trade Organisation – all wholly unelected people.

The House will forgive me for quoting myself, but in the course of my life I have developed five little democratic questions. If one meets a powerful person – Adolf Hitler, Joe Stalin or Bill Gates – ask them five questions: 'What power have you got? Where did you get it from? In whose interests do you exercise it? To whom are you accountable? And how can we get rid of you?' If you cannot get rid of the people who govern you, you do not live in a democratic system.

The role of the Speaker has another importance. When the political manifestos are yellowing in the public libraries, a good ruling from the Speaker in a footnote in Erskine May [*Treatise on the Laws, Privileges, Proceedings and Usage of Parliament*] might turn out to be one of the guarantees of our liberty.

There are two ways of looking at Parliament. I have always thought that, from the beginning – from the model Parliament – the establishment has seen Parliament as a means of management: if there is a Parliament, people will not cause trouble, whereas, of course, the people see it as a means of representation. Those are two quite different concepts of what Parliament is about. The establishment wants to defuse opposition through Parliament; the people want to infuse Parliament with their hopes and aspirations.

I have put up several plaques – quite illegally, without permission; I screwed them up myself. One was in the broom cupboard to commemorate Emily Wilding Davison, and another celebrated the people who fought for democracy and those who run the House. If one walks around this place, one sees statues of people, not one of whom believed in democracy, votes for women, or anything else. We have to be sure that we are a workshop and not a museum.

My next point, if I am not out of order, is that all progress comes, in my judgement, from outside the House. I am in no way an academic, but if I look back over history, I see many advances first advocated outside the House, denounced by people in power and then emerging. Let me use a couple of non-controversial examples. Twenty years ago, Swampy would have been denounced as a bearded weirdy; he will probably be in the next honours list, because the environmental movement has won. Similarly, when that madman, Hamilton, killed the children at Dunblane, the then Conservative Home Secretary banned handguns within six months, because public opinion had shifted. So we are the last place to get the message, and it is important that we should be connected effectively to public will.

There is a lot of talk about apathy, and it is a problem, but it is two-sided. Governments can be apathetic about the people, as well as people being apathetic about governments. For me, the test of an effective, democratic Parliament is that we respond to what people feel in a way that makes us true representatives. The real danger to democracy is not that someone will burn Buckingham Palace and run up the red flag, but that people will not vote. If people do not vote, they destroy, by neglect, the legitimacy of the government who have been elected.

May I finish with a couple of personal points? I first sat in the Gallery sixty-four years ago, and my family have been here since 1892 and I love the place. I am grateful to my constituents who have elected me. I am grateful to the Labour Party, of which I am proud to be a member. I am grateful to the socialists, who have helped me to understand the world in which we live and who give me hope. I am also deeply grateful to the staff of the House – the clerks, the policemen, the security staff, the doorkeepers, librarians, Hansard and catering staff – who have made us welcome here.

May I finish, in order, by saying something about yourself, Mr Speaker? In my opinion, you are the first Speaker who has remained a Back-Bencher. You have moved the Speaker's Chair on to the Back Benches. You sit in the Tea Room with us. You are wholly impartial, but your roots are in the movement that sent you here, and you have given me one of the greatest privileges that I have ever had – the right to use the Tea Room and the Library after the election. Unless someone is a Member or a peer, he or she cannot use the Tea Room or the Library, but you have extended the rules by creating the title of 'Freedom of the House', so that the Father of the House and I will be able to use the Tea Room. You will not be shot of us yet. I hope in paying you a warm tribute, Mr Speaker, that you do not think that I am currying favour in the hope that I might be called to speak again because, I fear, that will not be possible.

8

Socialism

*The ideas at the heart of socialism go back to the beginning of
time and have found their advocates in every generation. The
Conservative governments of the 1980s, under Margaret Thatcher,
unleashed a ruthless and militant capitalism that challenged socialist
ideas inside and outside Parliament. I made several speeches in the
Commons to combat the ideology that enabled market forces
and state power to destroy the miners and the power of
workers, through their unions.*

HOUSE OF COMMONS DEBATE ON A MOTION OF NO
CONFIDENCE IN THE GOVERNMENT, 22 NOVEMBER 1990

This debate is long overdue. It gives the House an opportunity to
look back over a decade of Conservative government. The
Conservatives have had strong messages from their supporters and
from the electors suggesting that they cannot win with the leader

who they have so loyally supported. We shall vote for a motion of no confidence, but the Conservative Party has already had its motion of no confidence. I do not believe that we should attach that motion to the personality of the Prime Minister because it is the policies that she has pursued, not her style, which have led to the message from the British people. I do not believe in scapegoats and it is important that we should understand that every present and former member of the Cabinet, every Conservative Member of Parliament who has trooped through the Lobby night after night after night in support of those policies, every newspaper that has supported the government and every voter who voted for them share responsibility for the current situation.

So much has been said about the past that I want to speak about the future, but it would be wrong to let the motion of censure go by without touching on some of the damage that has been done in the past decade. I must admit that the mechanical recitation of statistics does not get near the real world.

One important point about which we rarely hear is that Britain has spent far too much money on defence and not enough on its industrial development. There is the illusion that the only reason for change in Eastern Europe is Britain's possession of a nuclear weapon. Is it honestly believed by any serious person that there would have been no demand for liberty in Poland, Hungary and the Soviet Union unless we had had a nuclear weapon from the United States? But the price we paid for that high defence expenditure has crippled our capacity to make and sell what is needed.

Despite the fact that we have been told that this is an entre-preneurial society, Britain has an utter contempt for skill. If one talks to people who dig coal and drive trains, or to doctors, nurses, dentists or toolmakers, one discovers that no one in Britain is interested in them. The whole of the so-called entrepreneurial society is focused on the City news that we get in every bulletin, which tells us what has happened to the pound sterling to three decimal points, against the basket of European currencies. Skill is what built this country's strength, but it has been treated with contempt . . .

Assets were built up by the labour of those who work in the electricity industry and by the taxpayer who invested in the equipment. Those assets are now to be auctioned at half their value to make a profit, for a tax cut for the rich before the next General Election. If ministers were local councillors, they would be before the courts for wilful misconduct, but because they are ministers and because some of them later go on to the boards of the companies they privatised, they are treated as businessmen who know better how to handle those companies as members of the board of directors than allegedly they did as the ministers responsible.

Local government has been crippled. Across the river is the County Hall of London County Council – the seat of government of the greatest city in the world. It is empty and is to be sold because the government wanted to cripple local government, and they have. The poll tax, the centralisation of the business rate and the punishment of Liverpool and Lambeth councillors were designed to take all power from local government and to put it in the hands of the government who claimed that they did not believe in the role of the state. Many people – I am one of them – feel strongly about the undermining of the trade unions, who now have fewer rights than their counterparts in Eastern Europe, the tax cuts for the rich and the benefit cuts for the poor, the censorship of the media, the abuse practised by the security services, the restriction on civil liberties, the

Falklands War and now the government's readiness to send more troops, announced today, to the Middle East to die for the control of oil. When we look back at the 1980s we see many victims of market forces. I do not share the general view that market forces are the basis of political liberty. Every time I see a homeless person living in a cardboard box in London, I see that person as a victim of market forces. Every time I see a pensioner who cannot manage, I know that he is a victim of market forces. The sick who are waiting for medical treatment that they could receive quicker through private insurance are victims of those same market forces.

The Prime Minister is a great ideologue. Her strength was that she understood a certain view of life, and when she goes there will be a great ideological vacuum. It is no good saying that we shall run market forces better than she did, because her whole philosophy was that one should measure the price of everything, but the value of nothing. We must replace that philosophy.

Mr Gorbachev and Mr Walesa must be more worried than anyone to discover that the Prime Minister on whom they have modelled their economic policy has collapsed at the very moment she had persuaded them that that was the way forward to political success. To put it crudely, the Berlin Wall has fallen in London today and changes will be made which will go further than the Conservative Party yet realises.

It is important to put on the record all those people who have been denounced in the past ten years as loonies, extremists and as the 'enemy within'. They saw earlier than others the meaning behind the government's policies. They include the miners and the miners' wives, who fought against the injustice of closing pits and going for nuclear power and imported coal . . . They include the Greenham Common women. I was in court when those women were charged with action likely to cause a breach of the peace. They were outside the camp, while inside were enough nuclear weapons to destroy humanity. They were the pioneers of the defeat of the Prime Minister . . .

What about the ambulance workers and the print workers at Wapping, the single-parent mothers, the greens and the people who came to Trafalgar Square on 31 March for the poll-tax demonstration? They reflect what the Henley candidate [Michael Heseltine] picked up and tried to use at a later stage to his advantage. The teachers and those who tried to defend the National Health Service were all grouped together as the enemy within. In fact, they were the first carriers of the message that the Tory Party has finally got . . .

I have a Measure called the Margaret Thatcher (Global Repeal) Bill which, if we got a majority, could go through both Houses in twenty-four hours. It would be easy to reverse the policies and replace the personalities – the process has begun – but the rotten values that have been propagated from the platform of political power in Britain during the past ten years will be an infection – a virulent strain of right-wing capitalist thinking which it will take time to overcome.

One cannot change human nature. There is good and bad in everybody, and for ten years the bad has been stimulated and the good denounced as lunatic, out of touch, cloud-cuckoo-land, extremist and militant. The Conservatives in power have been the cause of that. They do not quite yet know what has happened. They think that they are witnessing the retirement of a popular headmistress under circumstances that some might regret. In fact, they have killed the source of their own philosophy and opened the way for different ideas.

We must now look to the 1990s and beyond. Most people have modest aspirations. They want useful work and a home to live in, and they would like good education for themselves and their children, with proper health care, decent pensions and peace and dignity when they are old. In a rich country – we are often told how rich we are – that should be available if the distribution of wealth were correct. With that in mind, let us look at the world today. America, which has 2 per cent of the world's population, uses 25 per cent of the world's resources. For how long can that last? One does not need a Saddam Hussein or a Gaddafi to point out that maldistribution of wealth is the greatest source of international conflict. So we must look to a United Nations that is not just there to launch a war under American auspices, but is there to solve the problems that lead to war. It must help to redistribute the resources of the world.

I must speak about Europe because, after all, we are all Europeans. But I will not give up the right of the people whom I represent to decide the laws under which we are governed. I will not do that, and I have no right to do so. I only borrowed my powers from Chesterfield, and at the end of five years I must hand them back. It will be no good my saying, 'I am handing back some of them. The rest I gave to Europe.'

We must shift the money from weapons to development. We must protect the planet from the dangers that are associated with nationalism, fundamentalism, particularism and racism, for those, combined with nuclear and chemical weapons, could destroy the human race.

HOUSE OF COMMONS DEBATE ON THE ANNOUNCEMENT
OF A PROGRAMME OF SUBSTANTIAL PIT CLOSURES,
21 OCTOBER 1992

*I won the Chesterfied by-election on the day that the miners' strike of
1984 began, and became very involved in the miners' battles,
Chesterfield being at heart a mining town. The strike was engineered
by the Conservative government, which was determined to destroy the
National Union of Mineworkers and the power of trade unions and
to nullify Britain's dependence on its own energy sources. Once the
strike was over, successive Conservative governments closed down
Britain's coal mines and passed anti-trade-union legislation.*

Entirely lacking from the Conservative Party has been any awareness of the sense of public outrage that people could be treated
as the President of the Board of Trade [Michael Heseltine] did
when he announced the closure of thirty-one pits. Of course, individual Members may take a different view, but I say that it was
callous and brutal. That treatment came from a party that prides
itself upon a Citizens' Charter and a classless society. That is why
hundreds of thousands are marching in London today.

All my right hon. and hon. Friends know that these events are
part of a sustained attack upon the mining industry. It is taking
place because the previous Prime Minister [Margaret Thatcher]
regarded the National Union of Mineworkers as the 'enemy
within'. That term was coined for that reason. It gives me huge
pleasure that the Tory Party threw out Thatcher and the miners
re-elected Scargill. That man told the truth, and truth still has
value in the politics of our society when all the lies, half-truths
and half-promises about independent reviews are dismissed.

The President of the Board of Trade said that he agonised over the decision that was before him. He is not the one who will suffer agony if pits are closed. If he agonised, why did he not have a review during that process? If there had been a review, others could have submitted other views while his discussions took place.

I have a letter that came from the office of Cecil Parkinson when he was Energy Secretary. It is a response to someone who wrote from Derbyshire, and states that the privatisation of the electricity industry will have no effect on pit closures. Ministers have lied, lied and lied again about the mining industry. That is why people are so incensed.

Do not tell us that this is all about market forces. If those forces applied to the farming industry, half the farms in Britain would have closed years ago. We could get cheaper food from New Zealand and Australia. Of course, the Tory Party depends on the farmers and so it supports them. I am not in favour of applying market forces to farms. It is not possible to close a farm one year and open it the following year. We all know that the miners have not received set-aside grants. They have not been given money to stop producing coal. That is the reality of the debate . . .

I am intensely proud that I had a role to play in the energy policy of the Labour government. That government authorised the Selby project, as we authorised the Drax B coal-fired power station. We encouraged forty-two million tonnes of extra capacity to be found. Selby was opened and there was an assisted-burn scheme. We recognised that the then Central Electricity Generating Board needed a small grant to change the merit order of the power stations so that more coal could be burned. We introduced earlier retirement for miners, something for which they had pressed for a long time. We then – [*Interruption*] Closures took place after negotiation and agreement. They concentrated mainly on pit exhaustion and dangerous working. As the then Secretary of State, I offered the NUM a veto on all closures. I discovered that Australian coal had been imported on the instruction of the now Lord Walker when he was Secretary of State for Energy. When it arrived it was so expensive that the Generating Board sold it to France at a loss.

We require a re-examination of energy policy that brings fuel suppliers, fuel industries, customers and unions together. There was such a re-examination from 1976 onwards; the papers were published and the discussions were serious. When that process takes place, it will be necessary to determine the objectives of the energy policy, and one of the objectives of the Labour government was extremely simple. It was that everyone should have heat and light at home. That was not a bad energy-policy objective. It was a recognition of the fact that in the end an energy policy is judged by whether people can get hold of energy.

It has been said, 'If there is surplus coal, why not give it to pensioners?' That is a sensible argument. Coal could be supplied free of charge to the generators to pump it down the wire, as it were, in the form of cheap electricity. There are those who shake their heads in dissent, but that is an energy policy. It is one in which Conservative Members do not believe, because they believe in profit and not in people. That is what the argument is about.

We must think about imports and open-cast mining . . .

The environment of a village is destroyed by stripping it, as it were, for open-cast mining. We must have regard also to desulphurisation, assisted-burn and winter-fuel concessions. As many have said, how can we justify subsidy by way of the nuclear levy, a fuel that is three times as expensive as coal?

The House should not think that that for which I am arguing cannot be done. In 1945, Winston Churchill as Prime Minister, a distinguished predecessor, presented the Fuel and Power Act – I operated under it and so does the President of the Board of Trade – which, when enacted, charged the Secretary of State with the general duty of securing the effective and coordinated development of coal, petroleum and other mineral resources – fuel and power – in Great Britain. That is the statutory responsibility of the President of the Board of Trade. He is not merely a spectator of market forces. Indeed, in 1973 he was a member of a government who introduced the Fuel and Electricity Control Act, which bore on every fuel transaction in the country. When the right hon. Gentleman was a junior minister he controlled the supply of fuel to the aircraft industry. The result of tonight's Division will not determine the issue that is before us. If anyone thinks that it will, he or she is making a great mistake. In fact, the British public have been awakened to the realities of the mining industry and to the rotten philosophy of the 1980s. We were told that everything was about cash, and that chartered accountants had to be brought in to tell us what to do. That is not what it is all about. The issue is whether our society puts people in a place of dignity and serves them or whether we hand over money to gamblers who create no wealth.

What has happened – I warn the government about this – is that after ten years during which people took things that they should never have taken, there is a return of self-confidence and hope. It was that sort of self-confidence and hope that got Mandela out of prison and got the Berlin Wall down. Next it will get the President of the Board of Trade out of his office, in favour of a better society.

HOUSE OF COMMONS DEBATE ON SOCIALISM, 16 MAY 2000

On 23 April 1901, Keir Hardie, the then Member for Merthyr Tydfil, moved the following motion:

> That, considering the increasing burden which the private ownership of land and capital is imposing upon the industrious and useful classes of the community, the poverty and destitution and general moral and physical deterioration resulting from a competitive system of wealth production which aims primarily at profit making, the alarming growth of trusts and syndicates able by reason of their great wealth to influence Governments and plunge peaceful Nations into war to serve their interests, this House is of the opinion that such a condition of affairs constitute a menace to the well-being of the Realm, and calls for legislation designed to remedy the same by inaugurating a Socialist Commonwealth founded upon the common ownership of land and capital, production for use and not for profit, and equality of opportunity for every citizen [*Official Report*, 23 April 1901; vol. 92, c. 1175].

I had asked for a debate on socialism, but I was summoned to the Table Office and told that as no one had ministerial responsibility for socialism, it would have to be about wealth and poverty in the economic system. A Treasury minister has obligingly attended.

I want to look back to the roots of socialism, to celebrate what it is about and to see what relevance it may have to today's society. In doing so, I am bound to refer to some of its origins. The Bible has led to many revolutionary ideas – for instance, that we were and are all equal in the sight of God – which is why, in 1401, the House of Commons passed the Heresy Act, which condemned any lay person reading the Bible to be burned at the stake for heresy. The Bible has always been a controversial document. At the time of the Peasants' Revolt and the English revolution, people started thinking of common ownership, based on the life of the apostles.

Socialism is essentially about the moral values that guide society, about democracy and about internationalism. Its history in England is interesting to me because it goes back deep into the past. In 1832 . . . only 2 per cent of the population, all rich men, had the vote. The progress associated with socialism since then includes the Rochdale pioneers, who believed in cooperation; Robert Owen, the first man to call himself a socialist; the birth of the trade-union movement, when the Combination Acts were repealed; the Chartists, and later the suffragettes, demanding the vote; the demand for representation in Parliament through a Labour representation committee; and, finally, the idea that if people had the vote, they would have some democratic control over the economy as well as the political system.

If one considers the ideology or the basis of those ideas, Adam Smith and Karl Marx had something in common. Adam Smith said that the rich are the pensioners of the poor; that the rich live off the back of the poor. I do not want to shock the Chamber, but Karl Marx – the first philosopher to study British capitalism – identified a marginal difference of economic interests between those who slogged their guts out creating the wealth and those who happened to own it. Both believed in self-organisation.

The programme of socialism is sometimes associated with nationalisation. Nothing could be further from the truth. The first nationalised industry in Britain was the Church of England, which was nationalised by Henry VIII. Next, Charles II nationalised the Post Office. When I was Postmaster General, I wondered why. I found that he wanted to open everyone's letters, and he could do that only by creating the Royal Mail.

In June 1914, Winston Churchill nationalised British Petroleum. He paid £2 million for a commanding majority shareholding because he thought that the oil should be in the hands of the people. The BBC was nationalised by the Conservative Party. Imperial Airways was nationalised by the Conservative Party. The Army and the police, both of which are nationalised, have no relation with socialism whatever. I hope that Members will put out of their mind the idea that socialism is about running everything from the top.

The idea of socialism is of common ownership and that things are best done by cooperation. The Co-operative movement was based on that principle. Municipal ownership is a form of socialism. I pay tribute to the Liberal Party, which, in the nineteenth century – when Joseph Chamberlain ran Birmingham – introduced the municipal ownership of housing, gas, electricity, transport, opera, art galleries and airports. I learned to fly at the municipal airport in Birmingham.

The idea evolved that poor people, who could not afford by their own wealth to acquire the things that they needed – education, health, housing and transport – could buy them with their votes. The welfare state was the final development of this idea. In fairness to Lloyd George, the Budget that he introduced as Liberal Chancellor of the Exchequer laid the foundations of the pension system.

Although socialism is widely held by the establishment to be outdated, the things that are most popular in British society today are little pockets of socialism, where areas of life have been excluded from the crude operation of market forces and are protected for the benefit of the community.

One of the great impetuses in the post-war years for the advance towards the welfare state – with its socialist inspiration – was the argument, which I remember well because I made it myself, that if the nation could plan for war, it could plan for peace. We had full employment during the war. If we could plan to have full employment to kill people, why could we not plan to have full employment in peacetime, and so be able to build the houses and provide all the nurses and teachers that we needed? This idea was strongly entrenched and was in some ways non-controversial.

What might be called 'caring conservatism' – I use the phrase in a general spirit – was the idea in the minds of Winston Churchill and, before him, Harold Macmillan in the 1930s with his book *The Middle Way*. The idea was carried on by the right hon. Member for Old Bexley and Sidcup [Sir Edward Heath]. The right hon. Gentleman's powerful words, the 'unacceptable face of capitalism', were spoken by a Conservative Prime Minister. That may cause some concern to some of his supporters, but that is what he believed.

If one looks at the people who have described themselves as socialists in the last century, one finds two different types. I have mentioned what we were able to achieve in this country guided by the ideas that I have outlined. The Soviet Union had no democratic basis whatever for its socialism. It was born in revolution and suffered greatly in the war. In the end, the Soviet Union crumbled because, although the Soviet Communist Party, which called itself socialist, was overwhelmingly the largest party, it did not have the consent of the people.

The other type are the Social Democrats, who abandoned socialism altogether. The most powerful advocates of capitalism today are to be found among the Social Democrats. I do not want to be controversial, but it is a fact that there are no more powerful advocates of market forces and globalisation than those in the party that describes itself as New Labour.

Although globalisation has brought a great deal of industrialisation, it has also produced acute poverty in the Third World. The gap between rich and poor is wider now than a hundred years ago. There is the grossest exploitation of people in Third World countries. People here can invest their capital in the Third World, where wages are lower, and then lay off people in Britain – who then go on to unemployment benefit – and make their profits in much poorer countries.

Globalisation is said to be a form of internationalism. However, capital can be exported to another country to benefit from lower wages, but people from other countries who want to come here to benefit from increased wages are shut out by immigration laws. It is a limited, one-sided form of globalisation. Conflicts as deep as those that are caused by the division of wealth and poverty inevitably lead to war.

We made great advances towards democracy from 1832 to the end of the European empires and the creation of the welfare state, but the power in a globalised economy is unaccountable. Major multinational companies are not accountable to the people whom they employ or to the nations in which they work. I spent my life as a minister negotiating with oil companies and large multinationals that were more powerful than nation states. Indeed, they operated in this country like a colonial power.

Such activities have severe implications for our political system, and we must consider what has become of politics. The idea of representation has been replaced with the idea of management. I represent the interests of the people of Chesterfield as best I can and I also represent my convictions. People know what my convictions are when they vote and can get rid of me if they do not agree with them. But now we are all being managed on behalf of a global economy. Someone once said that, if we do not control the economy in the interests of the people, we have to control the people in the interests of the economy. That process is going on at a great pace.

We are told about our international competitors as if competition were at the core of a peaceful world; that is not a view that I share. The lack of accountability has a profound effect on the emerging democracies in the Third World. They are often denied the benefit of the hundreds of years of parliamentary experience from which we gained. However, even in this country, the power of the multinationals is increasingly becoming such that governments tremble before them. I was in the Cabinet in 1976 when we crumbled before the International Monetary Fund, which had serious consequences for the Party and the government.

We are now moving into another aspect of the political consequences of globalisation – the Third Way. The idea is that it would be better for all the good people at the top to get together. The project is a coalition of people who believe that there is a common view at the top, and that that is the only way in which to manage the economy. It is a one-party state. As a minister, I visited Moscow and met the Central Committee of the Communist Party and the commissars. They had not been elected. I then went to Brussels and met the commissioners. They had not been elected. I met representatives of the Central Bank. They, too, had not been elected. The reduction of democratic control as a result of globalisation is a serious problem, and Europe is part of it.

I fear the consequences that will arise if people do not believe that they are represented. One consequence is apathy. If people do not vote because they do not believe that it makes a difference, the consequences for the legitimacy of the government who win are profound. Low turnout is one aspect of that apathy. Clinton was elected by one in five of the American people; four out of five did not register, did not vote or voted against him. A low turnout, accompanied by cynicism, is a recipe for conflict and repression.

My age allows me to recall what happened in Germany before the war, where a despairing people turned to Hitler, who blamed the Jews and the trade unionists for their problems. He told the people that he would give them full employment, and by God he did – he rearmed them, and we had a war as a result.

It is necessary to say plainly and clearly that peace without social justice is impossible. We cannot have a peaceful society or a peaceful world if the principles of social justice are secondary to the search for profit. A society that is built around people and not profit is what lies at the heart of the socialist idea.

In the debate to which I referred at the outset of my remarks, Keir Hardie concluded, 'We are called upon at the beginning of the twentieth century to decide the question propounded in the Sermon on the Mount as to whether or not we will worship God or Mammon. The present day is a Mammon-worshipping age. Socialism proposes to dethrone the brutal god Mammon and to lift humanity into its place. [*Official Report*, 23 April 1901; vol. 92, c. 1179]

That is a very religious way of putting it, but it explains the idea that has moved people to do things. All real change comes from underneath. The idea of cooperation rather than competition appeals to most people in their own lives. Competition creates insecurity and anxiety, while cooperation is always dominant when people look after their disabled children or their old parents. I think that that idea is of value.

I want to leave time for what will be a full debate, so I shall conclude on the policies that may follow from the ideas that I have advanced. First, we must expand the public services and ensure that they are publicly funded. In the immediate post-war years, the idea of National Insurance was based on that of universal benefits. I do not believe that it is right for people to be means-tested before they are entitled to benefits for which they have paid, either through National Insurance contributions or taxation. That is especially true of the need to link pensions with earnings. I am proud to have been in the Cabinet that made that link and I am distressed that it was reversed, at a cost of about thirty pounds a week to pensioners. That provides a good example of what should be done.

We should have expanded public services for the provision of health care and education, which should be open, so as to allow every child access to the full range of knowledge in schools that are comprehensive in what they offer. Also, there should be access to the media, which does not usually cover the concerns of those who do not have wealth and power. I should add to that list the legal services, which are very expensive but absolutely necessary.

The second item on my list is the revitalisation of local government. I referred to the great Liberal achievements of the nineteenth century, and there are many examples of such achievements in the twentieth century. Local government should have the funding that it requires, the right to raise its own money – if it can persuade its electors to give it that money – and general powers that are not tied up by specific grants that local authorities administer but do not decide.

Thirdly, if we are genuinely interested in the idea of full employment, it is essential that we support manufacturing industry. For most of my life as a minister, I tried as best as I could – sometimes successfully, but generally not – to reverse de-industrialisation. In 1948, Britain launched 48 per cent of all the ships launched in the world. In 1970, we had the largest motorbike industry in the world. In 1974, we had the largest machine-tool industry and the largest car industry in Europe. That has all gone.

It is in the national interest to protect ourselves from invasion from abroad. We would resist anyone who tried to bomb our car factories, but if somebody buys and closes those factories, it is regarded as an inevitable consequence of globalisation. I do not think that that is a sustainable position. The same is true of privatisation. I hesitate to quote Harold Macmillan, but he said that privatisation was selling the family silver. That is not an example that would come immediately to mind for most families, but it was a vivid description of the sale of our natural assets.

We must have civil liberties. I refer not just to legal liberties and an end to discrimination, but to the acceptance of trade-union rights. It is amazing that we talk about a global economy, but that we do not legislate to implement the rights given to trade unions in the International Labour Organisation. I have introduced a Bill on the matter – the House may want to consider it – as such legislation is necessary.

We need a fairer tax system. I cannot understand why any government should ring-fence the rich and say, 'Whatever we do, we will not ask you to pay more', when people on benefits are continually being faced with demands to open the books and be examined, in an attempt to deal with benefit fraud. My hon. Friend the Member for North-East Derbyshire [Harold Barnes] may wish to raise the question of the Tobin tax, which would tax international transactions and could provide billions of pounds for international development.

It is often argued that no one has any power over multinationals, but I do not believe that. Multinational companies spend millions of pounds on trying to win popular support through advertising campaigns, because they know that it is necessary to retain the goodwill of host governments. I believe that it is necessary to treat multinationals as international agents and to negotiate with them as if they were countries.

We must have stronger environmental laws. Keir Hardie was a passionate environmentalist, who complained about the rain forests in the United States being cut down. He was also a great believer in animal rights. On one occasion, Hardie was followed home from the House of Commons by a journalist from the *Daily Mail*, who hoped to find out to whom he talked in the street – no doubt, in an attempt to uncover some scandal. The journalist said that Hardie patted all the horses that he saw in the street. Being a miner, Hardie appreciated the value of the pit pony.

We need to end the arms trade, which is far more serious than the drugs trade that receives so much attention. The arms trade allows arms manufacturers to arm both sides in a conflict. Then, when those arms are used, the world demands a ceasefire. I sometimes wonder whether the idea is to discover which arms work best so that more can be sold afterwards, as we saw in the case of the Exocet that sank HMS *Sheffield* during the Falklands War.

Finally, we should try to build the United Nations as an embryonic, democratic institution, in accordance with the aspirations of the Chartists, who wanted to establish democratic government in Britain. If we are to have a global system, it must be a world-wide system, but it must be based on democratic accountability. My conviction is that the UN is being bypassed by NATO, whereas the UN should have responsibility, through the General Assembly, for controlling multinationals, which cannot be disciplined in any other way. The World Trade Organisation and the IMF should also be accountable to the United Nations General Assembly. That would be true internationalism rather than globalisation.

Those are my convictions. I am a socialist and I became a socialist through experience. After fifty years in the House and many years as a minister, I realise the way in which power is exercised to shape our society. As I leave the House of Commons and approach a new political life at the end of this Parliament, I shall want to put those arguments to the electors as a non-candidate when the election comes, because I honestly believe that the ideas have much more support than the British establishment, any government or the House yet realises.

All progressive change has come from underneath, and it might be worth remembering that there is a different tradition from those ideas with which we are presented every day. If we remember that, we might make more progress in winning public support for what needs to be done.